The MIGHTY Accordion

A Complete Guide to Mastering Left-Hand Melodies, Walking Bass Lines, and Chord Progressions

VOLUME TWO

by David DiGiuseppe

Includes exercises designed to improve the accordionist's left-hand skills by:
Building finger strength and dexterity
Playing bass melodies and walking bass lines
Exploring contemporary chord progressions and 12 bar blues

For intermediate to advanced players

Audio tracks for all exercises available

www.melbay.com/31062MEB

WWW.MELBAY.COM

Contents

Accompanying Audio Tracks

Section 1

Track 1 - Exercise 1.1
Track 2 - Exercise 1.2
Track 3 - Exercise 1.3
Track 4 - Exercise 1.4
Track 5 - Exercise 1.5
Track 6 - Exercise 1.6
Track 7 - Exercise 1.7
Track 8 - Exercise 1.8
Track 9 - Exercise 1.9
Track 10 - Exercise 2.1
Track 11 - Exercise 2.2
Track 12 - Exercise 2.3
Track 13 - Exercise 2.4
Track 14 - Exercise 2.5
Track 15 - Exercise 2.6
Track 16 - Exercise 2.7
Track 17 - Exercise 2.8
Track 18 - Exercise 3.1
Track 19 - Exercise 3.2
Track 20 - Exercise 3.3
Track 21 - Exercise 3.4
Track 22 - Exercise 4.1
Track 23 - Exercise 4.2
Track 24 - Exercise 4.3
Track 25 - Exercise 4.4
Track 26 - Exercise 4.5
Track 27 - Exercise 4.6
Track 28 - Exercise 4.7
Track 29 - Exercise 5.1
Track 30 - Exercise 5.2
Track 31 - Exercise 5.3
Track 32 - Exercise 5.4
Track 33 - Exercise 5.5
Track 34 - Exercise 5.6
Track 35 - Exercise 5.7

Section 2

Track 36 - Exercise 6.1
Track 37 - Exercise 6.2
Track 38 - Exercise 6.3
Track 39 - Exercise 6.4
Track 40 - Exercise 6.5
Track 41 - Exercise 6.6
Track 42 - Exercise 6.7
Track 43 - Exercise 6.8
Track 44 - Exercise 6.9
Track 45 - Exercise 6.10
Track 46 - Exercise 6.11
Track 47 - Exercise 6.12
Track 48 - Exercise 7.1
Track 49 - Exercise 7.2
Track 50 - Exercise 7.3
Track 51 - Exercise 7.4
Track 52 - Exercise 7.5
Track 53 - Exercise 7.6
Track 54 - Exercise 7.7
Track 55 - Exercise 7.8
Track 56 - Exercise 7.9
Track 57 - Exercise 7.10
Track 58 - Exercise 7.11
Track 59 - Exercise 7.12
Track 60 - Exercise 8.1
Track 61 - Exercise 8.2
Track 62 - Exercise 8.3
Track 63 - Exercise 8.4
Track 64 - Exercise 8.5
Track 65 - Exercise 8.6
Track 66 - Exercise 8.7
Track 67 - Exercise 8.8
Track 68 - Exercise 8.9
Track 69 - Exercise 8.10

Section 3

Track 70 - Exercise 9.1
Track 71 - Exercise 9.2
Track 72 - Exercise 9.3
Track 73 - Exercise 9.4
Track 74 - Exercise 9.5
Track 75 - Exercise 9.6
Track 76 - Exercise 9.7
Track 77 - Exercise 9.8
Track 78 - Exercise 9.9
Track 79 - Exercise 9.10
Track 80 - Exercise 9.11
Track 81 - Exercise 9.12
Track 82 - Exercise 9.13
Track 83 - Exercise 9.14
Track 84 - Exercise 9.15
Track 85 - Exercise 9.16
Track 86 - Exercise 9.17
Track 87 - Exercise 9.18
Track 88 - Exercise 9.19
Track 89 - Exercise 9.20
Track 90 - Exercise 9.21
Track 91 - Exercise 9.22
Track 92 - Exercise 9.23
Track 93 - Exercise 9.24
Track 94 - Exercise 9.25
Track 95 - Exercise 9.26
Track 96 - Exercise 9.27
Track 97 - Exercise 9.28
Track 98 - Exercise 9.29
Track 99 - Exercise 9.30
Track 100 - Exercise 9.31
Track 101 - Exercise 10.1
Track 102 - Exercise 10.2
Track 103 - Exercise 10.3
Track 104 - Exercise 10.4
Track 105 - Exercise 10.5
Track 106 - Exercise 10.6
Track 107 - Exercise 10.7
Track 108 - Exercise10 8
Track 109 - Exercise 10.9
Track 110 - Exercise 10.10
Track 111 - Exercise 10.11
Track 112 - Exercise 10.12
Track 113 - Exercise 10.13
Track 114 - Exercise 10.14
Track 115 - Exercise 10.15
Track 116 - Exercise 10.16

Track 117 - Exercise 10.17
Track 118 - Exercise 10.18
Track 119 - Exercise 10.19
Track 120 - Exercise 10.20
Track 121 - Exercise 10.21
Track 122 - Exercise 10.22
Track 123 - Exercise 11.1
Track 124 - Exercise 11.2
Track 125 - Exercise 11.3
Track 126 - Exercise 11.4
Track 127 - Exercise 11.5
Track 128 - Exercise 12.2
Track 129 - Exercise 12.2
Track 130 - Exercise 12.3
Track 131 - Exercise 12.4
Track 132 - Exercise 12.5
Track 133 - Exercise 13.1
Track 134 - Exercise 13.2
Track 135 - Exercise 13.3
Track 136 - Exercise 13.4
Track 137 - Exercise 13.5
Track 138 - Exercise 13.6
Track 139 - Exercise 14.1
Track 140 - Exercise 14.2
Track 141 - Exercise 15.1
Track 142 - Exercise 15.2
Track 143 - Exercise 15.3
Track 144 - Exercise 16.1
Track 145 - Exercise 16.2
Track 146 - Exercise 16.3
Track 147 - Exercise 16.4
Track 148 - Exercise 16.5
Track 149 - Exercise 16.6
Track 150 - Exercise 16.7
Track 151 - Exercise 16.8
Track 152 - Exercise 17.1
Track 153 - Exercise 17.2
Track 154 - Exercise 17.3
Track 155 - Exercise 17.4
Track 156 - Exercise 17.5
Track 157 - Exercise 17.6
Track 158 - Exercise 17.7
Track 159 - Exercise 17.8
Track 160 - Exercise 17.9
Track 161 - Exercise 17.10
Track 162 - Exercise 17.11
Track 163 - Exercise 18.1
Track 164 - Exercise 18.2
Track 165 - Exercise 18.3
Track 166 - Exercise 18.4
Track 167 - Exercise 18.5
Track 168 - Exercise 18.6
Track 169 - Exercise 18.7
Track 170 - Exercise 18.8
Track 171 - Exercise 18.9
Track 172 - Exercise 18.10
Track 173 - Exercise 18.11

Track 174 - Ode to Joy (Pg. 28)
Track 175 - Down in the Valley (Pg. 28)
Track 176 - Wildwood Flower (Pg. 29)
Track 177 - Drink to Me with Only Thine Eyes (Pg. 30)
Track 178 - Spring (Pg. 30)
Track 179 - Auld Lang Syne (Pg. 31)
Track 180 - Amazing Grace (Pg. 33)
Track 181 - Come All Ye Fair and Tender Ladies (Pg. 34)
Track 182 - Simple Gifts (Pg. 34)
Track 183 - Jimmy Allen (Pg. 36)
Track 184 - The Star-Spangled Banner (Pg. 36)
Track 185 - Redwing (Pg. 37)
Track 186 - Nonesuch (Pg. 40)
Track 187 - Greensleeves (Pg. 41)
Track 188 - Down by the Riverside (Pg. 41)
Track 189 - On the Hills of Manchuria (Pg. 42)
Track 190 - Für Elise (Pg. 43)

Preface

Introduction

It is not uncommon for accordionists to possess considerable skill with the keyboard side of the instrument, but be limited to oom-pah-pah or simple accompaniment styles on the bass buttons. This guide addresses that imbalance.

The book's main objective is to elevate the player's left-hand abilities by significantly improving finger strength and dexterity, and increase the vocabulary of interesting and complex bass patterns. To do this, a series of graduated exercises teaches single note playing on the basses, then builds on those skills to create melodic and walking bass lines within harmonic passages. Along the way, the book examines numerous chord progressions commonly heard in popular music, helps improve note reading, and explores a variety of blues riffs. Thus, this material offers the accordionist a valuable tool to markedly advance mastery of left-hand technique.

About This Book

The book contains three sections. Section One is a short examination of bass/chord patterns. The initial exercises review basic concepts, but proceed quickly to more challenging material. The section's five chapters explore major chords, minor chords, the counter bass, seventh chords, and diminished chords respectively. This section is not meant to be an exhaustive tutor, but rather a review and preparation for the upcoming exercises.

Section Two focuses on playing melodies with the basses through a series of progressively more difficult exercises. The first two chapters present material in the keys of C, G, D, and F major, starting with simple scale-based patterns and proceeding to more challenging pieces. The section's final chapter contains a series of exercises specifically designed to strengthen the fifth finger, which is typically much weaker than its counterparts.

The emphasis of Section Three is on chord progressions. The section's first chapter presents numerous note patterns which can be played in the context of a single chord. The following eight chapters each present a different chord progression. The exercises explore the use of arpeggios and walking bass lines to connect chords, and integrate a variety of rhythmic patterns. The penultimate chapter surveys a number of chord progressions not covered in the preceding chapters. The final chapter presents numerous blues riffs played within the standard 12 bar blues format.

Accompanying Audio Files

Audio files of every exercise and song in this book are available for download. See page 4 for audio track numbers and corresponding music. In the files, each piece is played slowly. To practice while playing along with the files, the use of digital software with the ability to vary the music's tempo is recommended.

Whom the Book is For

This book is not intended to be a primer for beginner accordion students. The material assumes a basic knowledge of the accordion, the faculty to read music on at least a rudimentary level, and a capacity to play simple songs. For the accordionist with considerably more expertise, the book offers a valuable opportunity to practice new and unique bass patterns with the goals of significantly improving the left-hand's capabilities and advancing overall musicianship.

How to Use This Book

It is not essential to start at the beginning of this book. Given the progressive nature of these studies, the intermediate student can begin with the more advanced exercises. It may be useful, however, for all to review Section One which covers left-hand foundational skills.

At first, each exercise should be played slowly and accurately. Once it can be played correctly at a slow pace, the tempo can be increased. Use a metronome to ensure a steady tempo and to calibrate progress. Play each exercise no faster than it can be played correctly. It is a waste of valuable time to practice mistakes!

Bass Notation

Illustration 1 (page 8) shows the bass button configuration for a standard Stradella style 120 bass accordion. The buttons are arranged in six vertical columns with rows ordered in the circle of fifths.

The accordion's left-hand notation is written in the bass or F clef (see Illustration 2). Notes appearing on the staff from the center line down (with stem up) are single notes, played either in the bass or counter bass column. A short line placed under the note indicates it is to be played as a counter bass.

Notes placed on the third space or above (with stem down) represent chords. A superscript indicates which chord quality is to be played—M indicates major chord, m indicates minor chord, 7 indicates the seventh chord, and d indicates diminished chord.

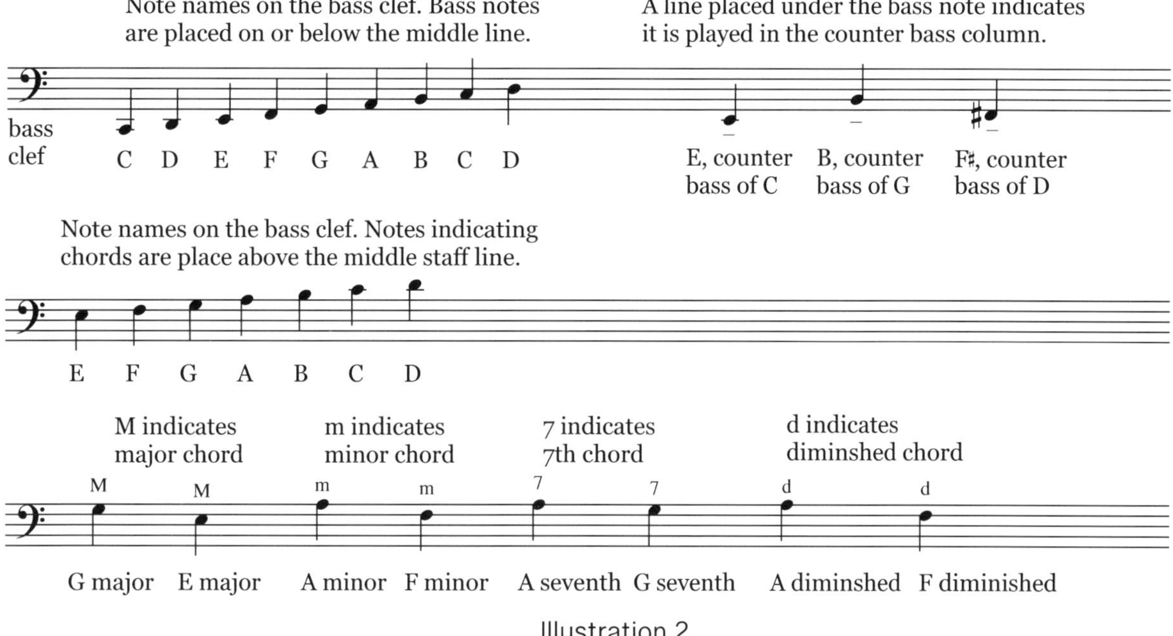

Illustration 2

Note—though this is the standard notation, there are a few exceptions to this convention in Sections Two and Three. In exercises where only melodies are played, with no chords present, the notes may be placed above the middle line and do not represent chords. In this case, there will be no chord quality indicated. Where appropriate, this will be noted in the text.

Left-Hand Fingering

4th Finger on Root Method

When playing typical bass/chord patterns, the fourth (ring) finger plays the root bass button. The third (middle) finger plays the major chord button. The second (index) finger plays the minor, seventh, and diminished chord buttons. The fourth finger also plays the counter bass button (see Illustration 3).

In an alternating bass pattern played with a major chord, the second finger plays the alternate bass. The third finger plays the alternate bass when using a minor or seventh chord.

Illustration 1
Notes and Chords on a Stradella style 120 Bass Accordion

On all accordions, the C bass button is physically marked, often with an indentation or rhinestone. On most accordions, the E and A♭ bass buttons are also marked.

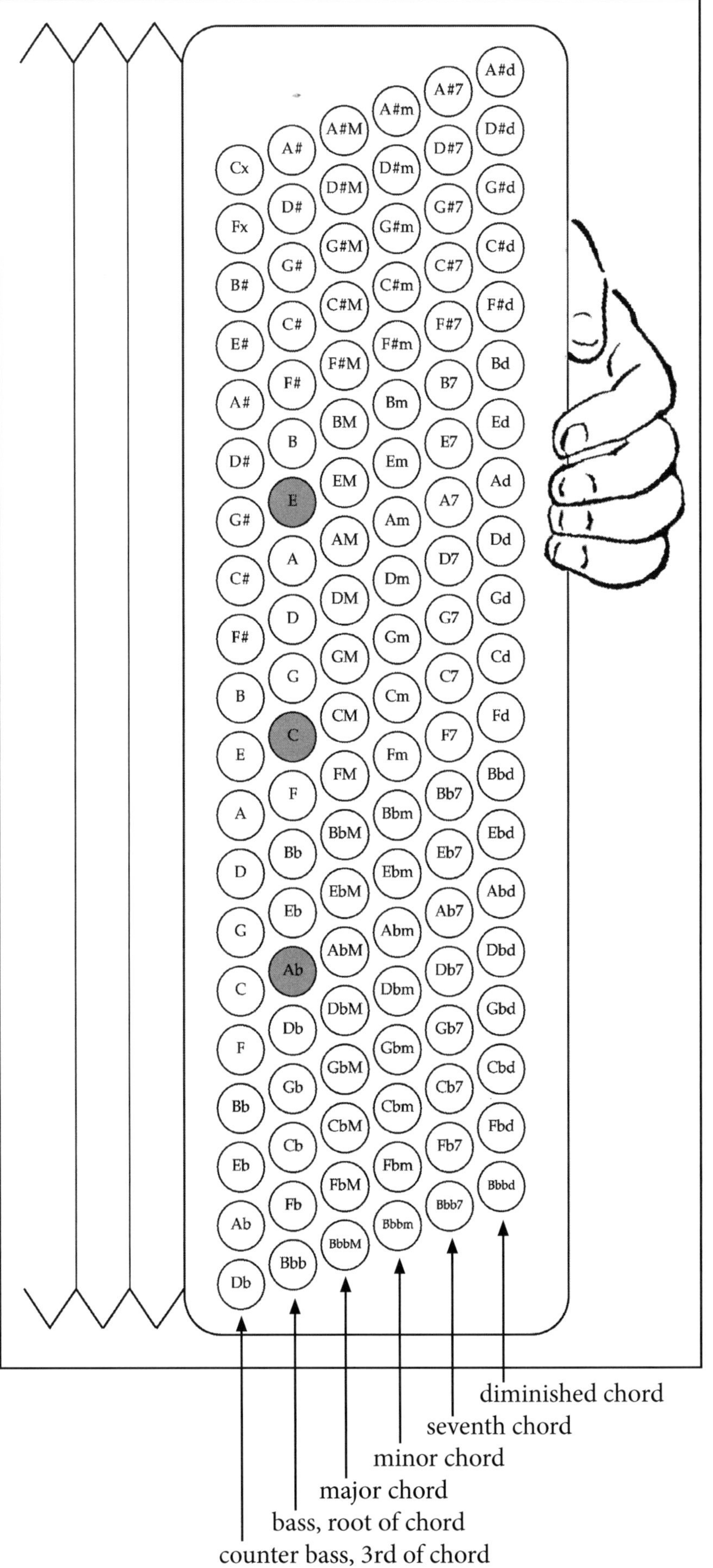

Note that these fingering positions are for playing bass/chord patterns. When playing melodic passages or walking bass lines with the left hand, these patterns are not necessarily engaged.

Fingering positions used to play typical bass/chord patterns.

Illustration 3

3rd Finger on Root Method

An alternative method is to use the third finger on the root bass button with the second finger on the major chord button.

This author has a strong preference for the fourth finger convention; consequently, all fingering suggestions in the book are consistent with this method.

Enharmonic Equivalents

Two notes playing the same pitch but with different names are said to be enharmonic equivalents (see Illustration 4). For example, G♯ and A♭ are the same pitch and therefore played with the same button. On the accordion's bass side, G♯ and A♭ can be played as the counter bass of E, or as the A♭ button in the bass column.

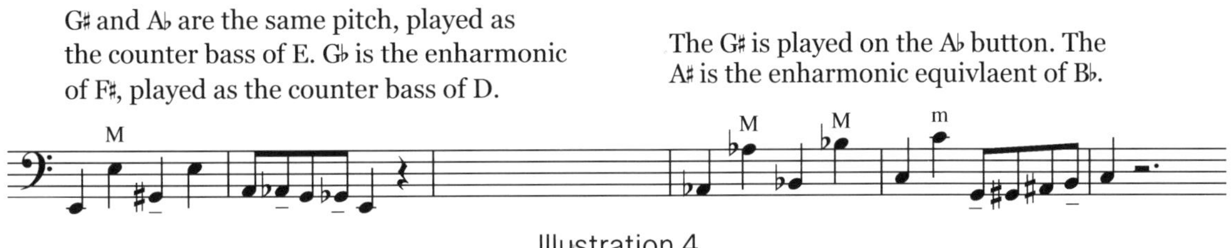

Illustration 4

Chord Numbering

Chords in any key can be assigned numbers based on the scale degree of the chord's root (see Illustration 5). For example, in the key of C, the C chord is the "one" or I chord. The fourth degree of the scale is F, hence the F chord is the IV chord. G, being the fifth degree of the scale, is the V chord.

Roman numerals can be used to identify the scale degree of chords. A major chord is indicated with an upper case Roman numeral. A lower case numeral indicates a minor or diminished chord.

Illustration 5

When a series of triads is written over each note only using the notes of that scale, the chords of the first, fourth, and fifth degrees are major (see Illustration 6). The chords of the second, third, and sixth degrees are minor. The seventh degree is diminished. Notice the relation of chords to Roman numeral cases.

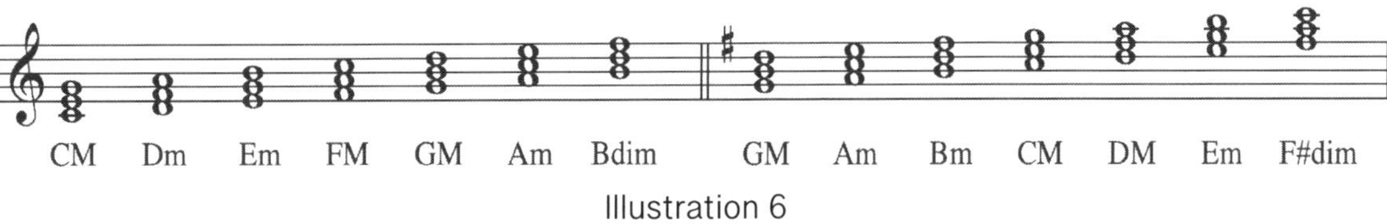

Illustration 6

The advantage of this system is that, though the chord names change with each key, the chord quality stays the same. Hence the I chord in any major key is always major. The ii chord is always minor, etc.

This provides a convenient way to refer to chord changes. The ii - V - I progression in the key of C major is Dm - G - C, while in G major it is Am - D - G. Harmonically, the two chord progressions function in the same way; they are just in different keys.

Roman numerals can further identify a chord's quality with additional symbols. V7 indicates a dominant seventh chord, such as C7 or G7. By contrast, iim7 indicates a minor seventh chord, such as Dm7 or Am7.

Syncopated Eighth Notes

Some exercises in this book are played with syncopated eighth notes. This swing feel, as it is often called, is executed with eighth notes alternating in duration long-short-long-short, etc. The time division between the long and short notes is not absolute, and varies subtly between musicians and music styles. The range of timing is between ♪.♬ ♪.♬ ♪.♬ ♪.♬ and ♩♪ ♩♪ ♩♪ ♩♪.

To indicate syncopated eighth notes, the symbol ♫ = ♩♪ is placed at the beginning of the exercise or song.

Acknowledgments

A mighty big THANK YOU to Bob Lijana and Nina Frankel for their invaluable insights and suggestions.

Section 1
Bass/Chord Patterns

Section 1 is a review of typical bass/chord patterns. The material covers the prerequisite skills and knowledge needed for the subsequent sections of this book. The exercises begin with the very basics of playing the accordion's bass side, but progress fairly quickly. If you are at a beginner level, and the exercises prove to be too difficult, it is recommended that you first work with *The Mighty Accordion Volume One—The Complete Guide to Mastering Left-Hand Bass/Chord Patterns* (Mel Bay Publications MB20740) which is a comprehensive skill-building tutor on bass/chord patterns.

Chapter 1

The Major Chord

We will start by playing bass notes and major chords. As mentioned in the preface, use your fourth finger on the bass note button and your third finger on the major chord. Your hand should feel secure between the accordion's side bass panel and the bass strap, but be able to move freely up and down. Keep your fingers curled and press the buttons with your fingertips. When releasing a button, be sure to keep your finger close to that button as you begin to play the next note. Train your fingers to minimize their movement, and avoid having your fingers rise or jump away from a button upon its release. Play each note staccato. And most importantly, be sure your shoulders, arms, and fingers stay relaxed.

Exercise 1.1 uses the C bass and C major chord buttons in a three-count pattern. When moving to the G, bring both fingers to the new position—fourth finger on the bass and third finger on the chord.

Exercise 1.1 - Audio track 1

Exercise 1.2 moves from the C to the G chords repeatedly. Pay attention to using the correct fingering as you move from one chord position to the next. In the last measure, the C bass note and C major chord buttons are pressed together and held for three counts.

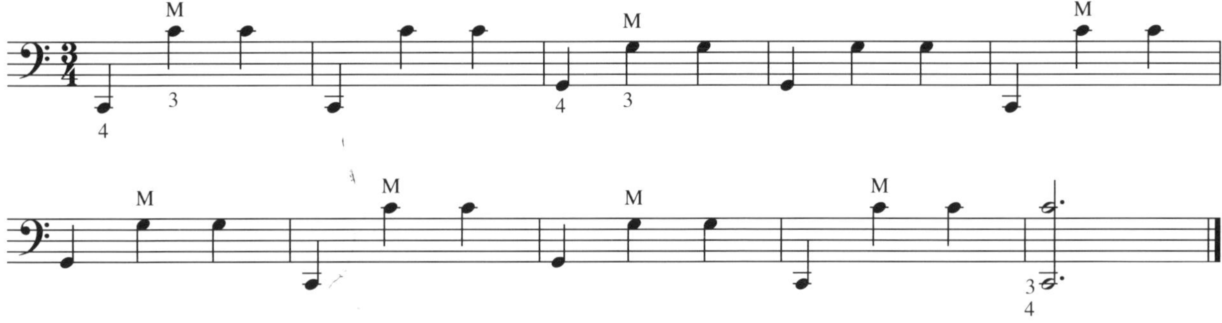

Exercise 1.2 - Audio track 2

Exercise 1.3 introduces the F bass and F major chord played in a four-count pattern.

Exercise 1.3 - Audio track 3

In Exercise 1.4, you will be moving between the G and F chord positions. Learn to jump directly from one row to the other without "feeling" your way across the C row buttons.

Exercise 1.4 - Audio track 4

Exercise 1.5 introduces the D bass and D major chord. Again, when moving between the D and C rows, practice moving your hand directly from one position to the other.

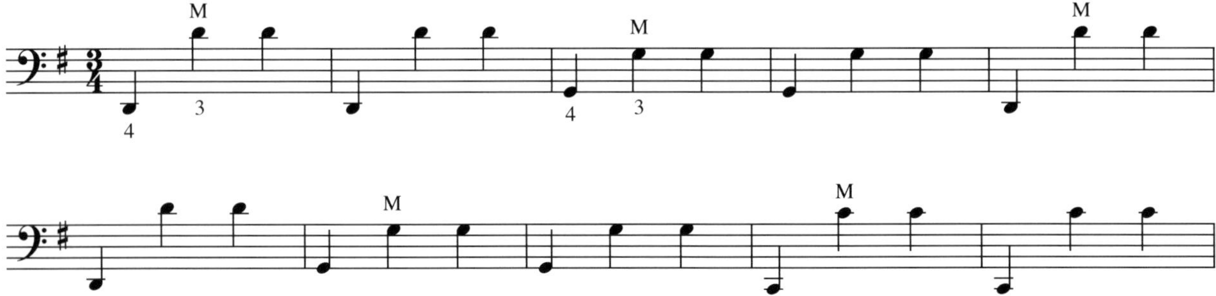

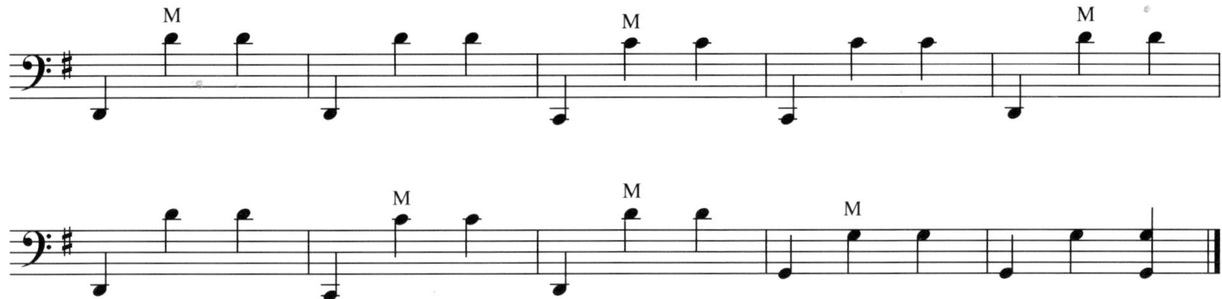

Exercise 1.5 - Audio track 5

Exercise 1.6 introduces the B♭ bass and major chord. Notice also that the three-count pattern is being altered, sometimes requiring the fourth finger to play consecutive notes while moving from one row to another. Be sure to maintain the hand position shape of the fourth finger on bass and the third finger on chord throughout the exercise. When playing B♭ to G—moving over two rows—practice jumping directly from one to the other.

Exercise 1.6 - Audio track 6

In Exercise 1.7, you will be playing bass and chord buttons together as you jump between rows. As in the previous exercises, use your four/three finger shape at all times.

Exercise 1.7 - Audio track 7

Exercise 1.8 introduces the alternating bass pattern with the major chord. The alternate is always the bass note in the above row. For the C position, the alternate bass is G. With your fourth finger on C bass and third finger on C major, use your second finger to play G, the alternate bass. In the G position, D is the alternate bass, played with the second finger. Learn to associate this hand shape with the major chord alternating bass pattern. Again, train your second finger to stay close to the buttons and not rise significantly after striking a note.

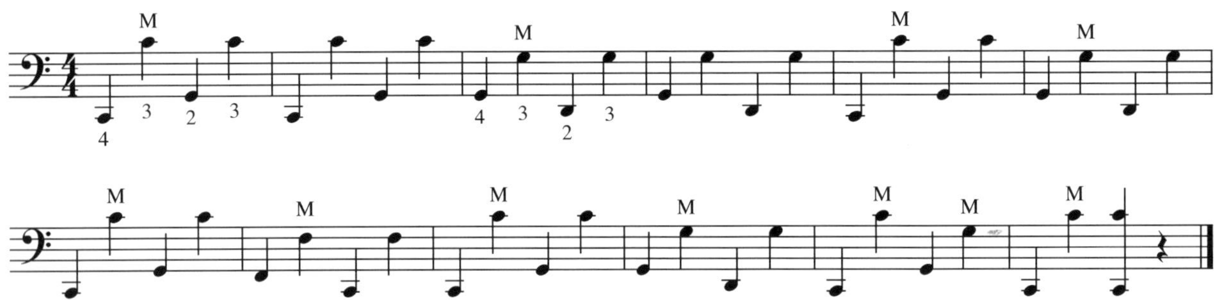

Exercise 1.8 - Audio track 8

Exercise 1.9 introduces the A bass and major chord, and their alternate bass E. There is also a jump from C to A, over two rows. Notice in measures 17, 19, and 21 the third note is not an alternate bass. Be sure to use the alternate bass shape to play the correct fingering in the last measure.

Exercise 1.9 - Audio track 9

Chapter 2

The Minor Chord

Exercise 2.1 introduces the C, F, and G minor chords. Use fingers four and two as indicated for the bass/ minor chord shape. Maintain use of this fingering throughout the exercise.

Exercise 2.1 - Audio track 10

Exercise 2.2 includes both minor and major chords. Be sure to use the correct fingerings. The fourth finger often plays consecutive notes while moving from one row to another.

Exercise 2.2 - Audio track 11

The chords in Exercise 2.3 jump around a bit more than in previous exercises. Practice moving directly between the B♭ major and G minor, jumping over two rows.

Exercise 2.3 - Audio track 12

Exercise 2.4 introduces the D and A minor chords, and includes a jump from A minor to F major, over three rows.

Exercise 2.4 - Audio track 13

Exercise 2.5 incorporates the E minor chord. In measures 5, 6, 7, 8, 10, 12, and 14, the bass note is held for all three counts within the measure as the chord is played on counts two and three.

Exercise 2.5 - Audio track 14

Exercise 2.6 introduces the alternating bass pattern with the minor chord. Use the third finger to play the alternate, with the fourth finger on the bass and second finger on the minor chord. Keep this shape as you move from one minor chord position to the next and when playing the last measure.

Exercise 2.6 - Audio track 15

Exercise 2.7 uses the E minor chord with its alternate bass B, and introduces the B minor chord with its alternate bass F♯.

Exercise 2.7 - Audio track 16

Exercise 2.8 uses the major and minor alternating basses in a three count pattern. Notice on the third count of measure 2 the fingering is altered from what has been used thus far. The third finger plays the A bass, instead of the fourth finger. This fingering allows for a smoother transition to the G, the first note of the next measure. Similarly, in measure 9 the third finger is used on the A bass note at count one instead of the fourth finger, again allowing for a smoother transition between measures 8 and 9. The transition between measures 12 and 13 employs the same technique. Notice also that the fingering in the last measure is modified from the standard pattern.

Exercise 2.8 - Audio track 17

Chapter 3

The Counter Bass

Exercise 3.1 introduces counter basses, which are the buttons of the inner-most column on the accordion's bass side (see Illustration 1, page 8). When playing bass/chord patterns, the counter bass is typically played with the fourth finger. The short line under the note indicates it is to be played as a counter bass. Notice that the first note (C) is written one octave higher than in previous exercises. On the accordion's bass, both notes are played with the same C bass button.

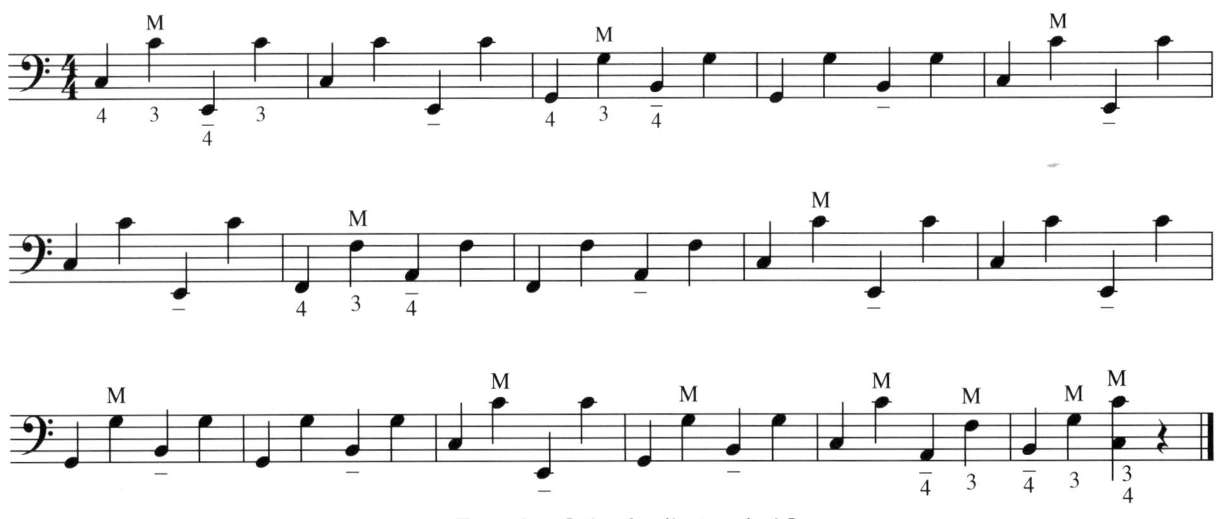

Exercise 3.1 - Audio track 18

Exercise 3.2 includes patterns using both counter and alternate basses. In measure 6, the alternate bass is played first. When moving from the previous D chord to measure 6, bring your whole hand into the A position, striking the counter bass first.

Exercise 3.2 - Audio track 19

Exercise 3.3 has its challenges. Notice where the suggested fingerings vary from the standard shape in order to facilitate a smoother transition from one note to another. In measure 20, the note D is played with the same button as D written an octave lower.

Exercise 3.3 - Audio track 20

Exercise 3.4 uses bass, alternate bass, and counter bass to play a descending and ascending scale.

Exercise 3.4 - Audio track 21

Chapter 4

The Seventh Chord

Exercise 4.1 introduces the seventh chord. Use the same 4/2 finger combination to play both the minor and the seventh chords with the root.

Exercise 4.1 - Audio track 22

Exercise 4.2 uses the seventh chord with both the alternate and the counter basses. With the fourth finger on the bass and the second finger on the seventh, the third finger plays the alternate bass. As with the major chord shape, the fourth finger is typically used to play the counter bass.

Exercise 4.2 - Audio track 23

Exercise 4.3 uses the seventh chord with both the alternate and the counter basses. In measures 4 and 11 the counter bass B can be referred to as a "leading tone" as it leads up to the C by the interval of 1/2 step. Can you find the other leading tone in this exercise?

Exercise 4.3 - Audio track 24

In Exercise 4.4, the standard major, minor, and seventh fingerings are sometimes altered to enable a smoother transition between notes.

Exercise 4.4 - Audio track 25

Exercise 4.5 is in a style called boogie blues (see Chapter 18). The symbol ♫ = ♩♪ (triplet) indicates eighth notes are to be played syncopated (see Syncopated Eighth Notes, page 10).

Exercise 4.5 - Audio track 26

In exercise 4.6, the standard major, minor, and seventh fingerings are again altered to enable a smoother transition between notes.

Exercise 4.6 - Audio track 27

There are numerous measures in exercise 4.7 where the alternate bass is played first. When coming from a different chord, remember to bring your hand into the appropriate position and shape as you play the first note of the alternating pattern.

Exercise 4.7 - Audio track 28

Chapter 5

The Diminished Chords

Exercise 5.1 introduces the diminished chord. When playing the diminished with the root, use the same 4/2 finger combination as when playing the minor and seventh chords.

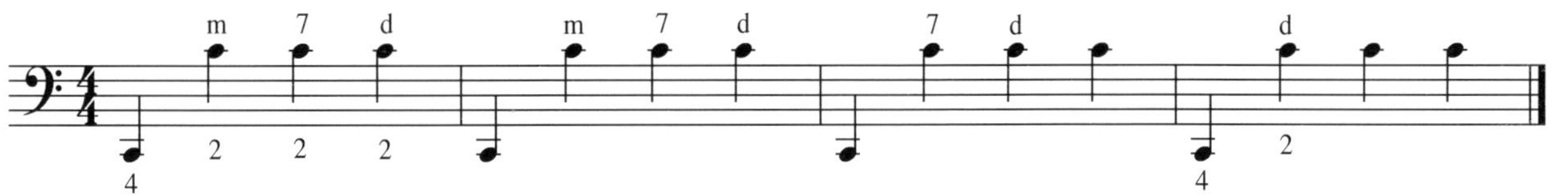

Exercise 5.1 - Audio track 29

Exercise 5.2 moves between major, minor, seventh, and diminished chords.

Exercise 5.2 - Audio track 30

Like above, exercise 5.3 encompasses major, minor, seventh, and diminished chords, but is a bit more challenging.

Exercise 5.3 - Audio track 31

Exercise 5.4 introduces the I - ♯i dim - ii - V7 chord progression. Since this exercise is in the key of C major, the I chord is C major, the #i dim is C# diminished, the ii chord is D minor, and the V7 chord is G seventh (see Chord Numbering, page 9). When employed this way, the diminished is considered a transition chord passing between the I to the ii chord. The chord changes in measures 1 through 10 are preparation for the full progression.

Exercise 5.4 - Audio track 32

Exercise 5.5 uses the diminished chord passing to the seventh chord, a progression occasionally found in blues and other genres.

Exercise 5.5 - Audio track 33

The diminished chord can also be used as a passing chord moving down by half steps, as shown in Exercise 5.6. The counter bass of A is C# and its enharmonic equivalent Db (see Enharmonic Equivalents, page 9). The chord changes in the first two lines are preparation for the full progression.

Exercise 5.6 - Audio track 34

In Exercise 5.7, the diminished is used as a transition chord to both move up and down between neighboring chords.

Exercise 5.7 - Audio track 35

Section 2
Bass Melodies

Section 2 focuses on playing melodies with the accordion's bass buttons. Practice these exercises diligently and by the section's end, your left-hand abilities will be greatly expanded.

We start with the C major scale and proceed to other keys as the chapters progress. The last chapter of this section focuses on strengthening the left hand's fifth finger.

Illustration 6.1 shows the notes and fingering of the C major scale.

Illustration 6.1

A helpful technique to playing scales and melodies is to recognize or "see" the shape of the scale—the relationship between the bass buttons and the fingering. Illustration 6.2 shows the buttons and fingerings used for the C major scale. Notice that the fourth finger plays the notes in the F row (F and its counter bass A), the third finger plays the notes of the C row (C and its counter bass E), and the second finger plays the notes in the G row (G and its counter bass B) plus the note D above G. This is the conventional major scale fingering, and can be visualized as a shape. One nice feature of the bass button's layout is that this shape of the major scale is the same regardless of which key it is played in. Of course, when playing a piece of music there will be many exceptions to this standard fingering. But knowing the shape offers a framework to start from.

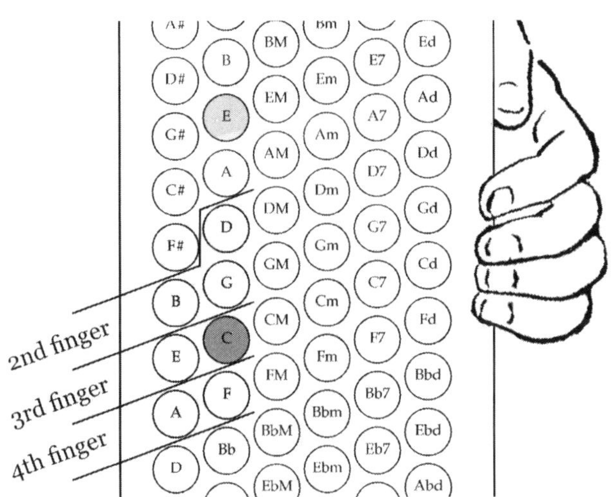

Illustration 6.2

Chapter 6

C and G Major Melodies

Exercise 6.1 presents the first four notes of the C major scale. Remember to use the correct fingering as you play through this and other exercises.

Exercise 6.1 - Audio track 36

Exercise 6.2 adds the notes G and A.

Exercise 6.2 - Audio track 37

Exercise 6.3 incorporates the note B. Remember that the note C in measures 4, 6, and 10, though written an octave above the starting C, is played with the same button.

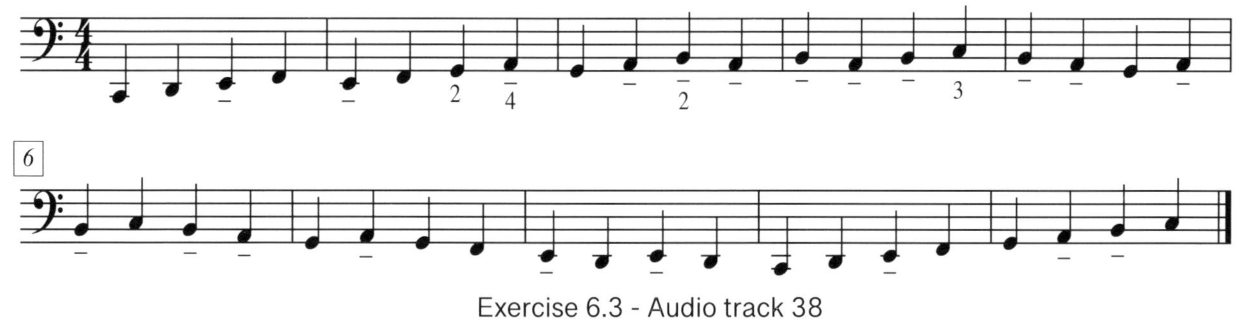

Exercise 6.3 - Audio track 38

Exercise 6.4 presents the C major scale played both ascending and descending.

Exercise 6.4 - Audio track 39

Exercises 6.5 and 6.6 use notes from the C major scale. Practice these exercises to learn the scale's shape.

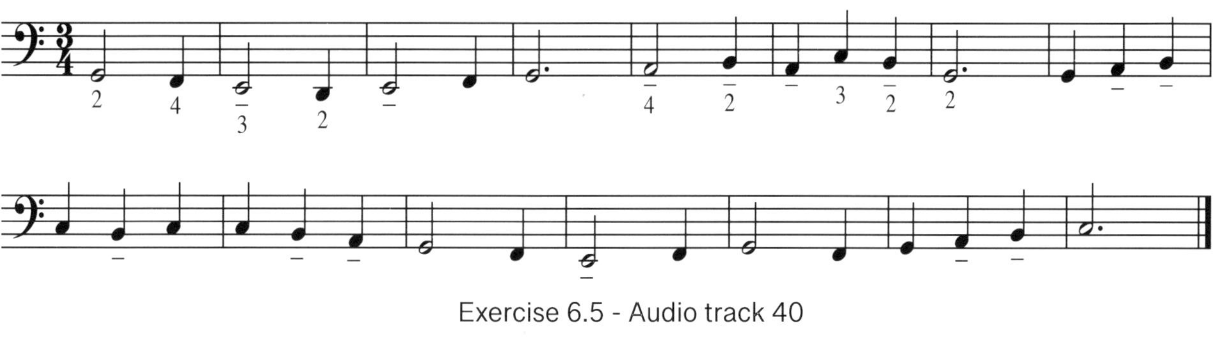

Exercise 6.5 - Audio track 40

Exercise 6.6 - Audio track 41

In measure 3 and elsewhere, Exercise 6.7 uses D counter bass of B♭. Notice in measures 3 and 4, the standard scale fingering is altered by placing the third finger on F in order to play the counter bass D. In measures 5 and 6, the fingering is again altered to eliminate playing three consecutive notes with the same finger. In measure 7, the fingering returns to the standard major scale shape. Notice also two new notes—D on the third staff line and E in the third space. Use the same buttons as their counterparts written an octave lower.

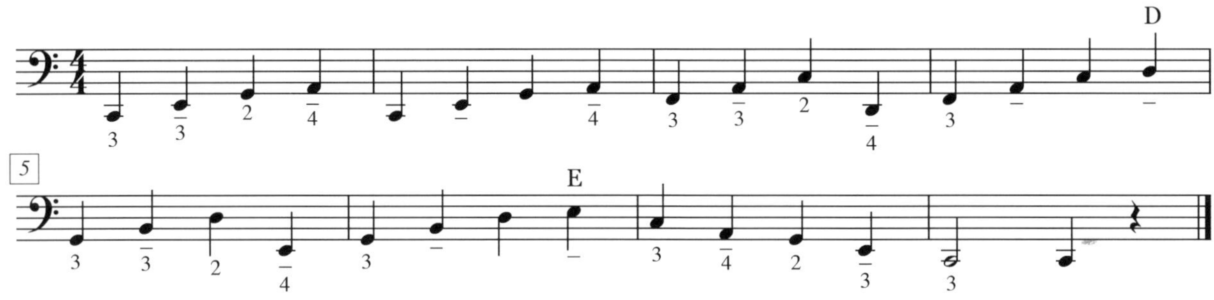

Exercise 6.7 - Audio track 42

For the following three songs, use the standard major scale fingering unless otherwise noted.

Ode to Joy

Ludwig van Beethoven

Audio track - 174

Down in the Valley

Audio track - 175

Wildwood Flower

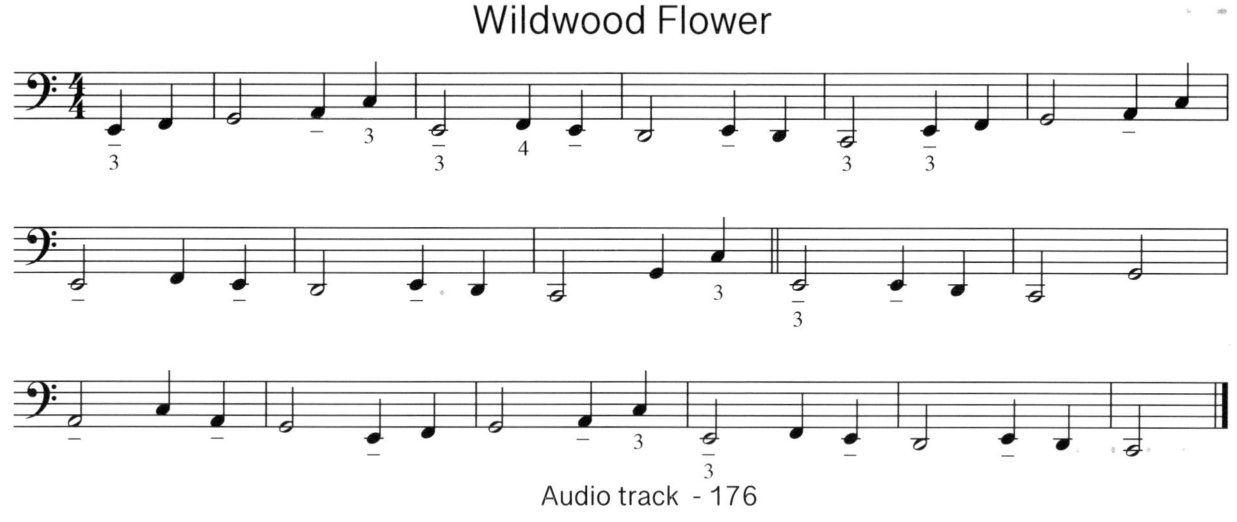

Audio track - 176

Exercises 6.8 introduces the G major scale. Use the same fingering pattern as the C scale.

Exercise 6.8 - Audio track 43

Exercise 6.9 is the same G scale as above. Though the notation is different, the fingering and bass buttons are the same. Notice the new notes F# and G.

Exercise 6.9 - Audio track 44

Exercise 6.10 uses the standard scale fingering except at the end to avoid using the same finger twice.

Exercise 6.10 - Audio track 45

Exercise 6.11 starts with the standard fingering, but as the exercise progresses alternate fingerings are used to facilitate smoother transitions between notes.

Exercise 6.11 - Audio track 46

Exercise 6.12 uses alternate fingerings for both smoother playing and, in measures 12 and 13, to avoid using the same finger on repeated notes.

Exercise 6.12 - Audio track 47

For the following three songs, use the standard major scale fingering unless otherwise noted.

Drink to Me with Only Thine Eyes

Audio track - 177

Spring

from The Four Seasons

A. Vivaldi

Audio track - 178

Auld Lang Syne

Audio track - 179

Chapter 7

D and F Major Melodies

Exercise 7.1 introduces the D major scale, with a key signature of F# and C#. C# is the counter bass of A. The E bass note is located above A. Use the standard major scale fingering starting on D.

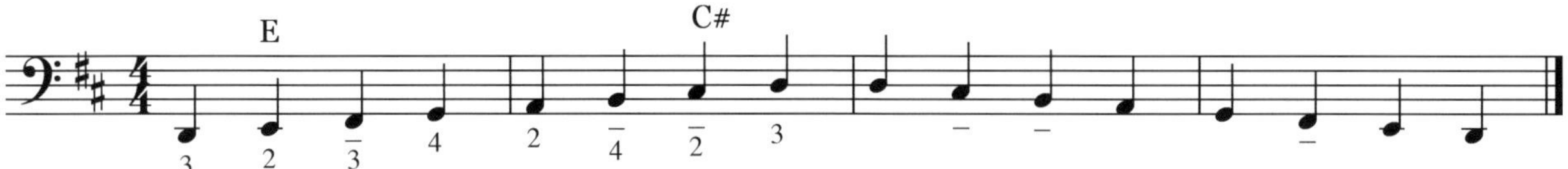

Exercise 7.1 - Audio track 48

Use the standard major scale fingering for Exercise 7.2.

Exercise 7.2 - Audio track 49

Exercise 7.3 alters the standard fingering in a few passages for smoother transitions between notes.

Exercise 7.3 - Audio track 50

Exercise 7.4 uses the standard scale shape until the last few measures.

Exercise 7.4 - Audio track 51

Exercise 7.5 uses the standard fingering except where noted.

Exercise 7.5 - Audio track 52

Measure 3 of Exercise 7.6 uses the same fingerings as the previous two measures, though playing different notes. Keep your hand in the same shape as you move between measures 2 and 3. Measure 5 is also played with the same fingering pattern. Again, move your hand and maintain the shape. This shape is also used elsewhere in the exercise. Notice the E's in measures 11 and 12 are played as counter basses. B in measure 15 is above E and played in the bass column.

Exercise 7.6 - Audio track 53

The following three songs are in the key of D major. Use the standard scale fingering unless otherwise noted.

Amazing Grace

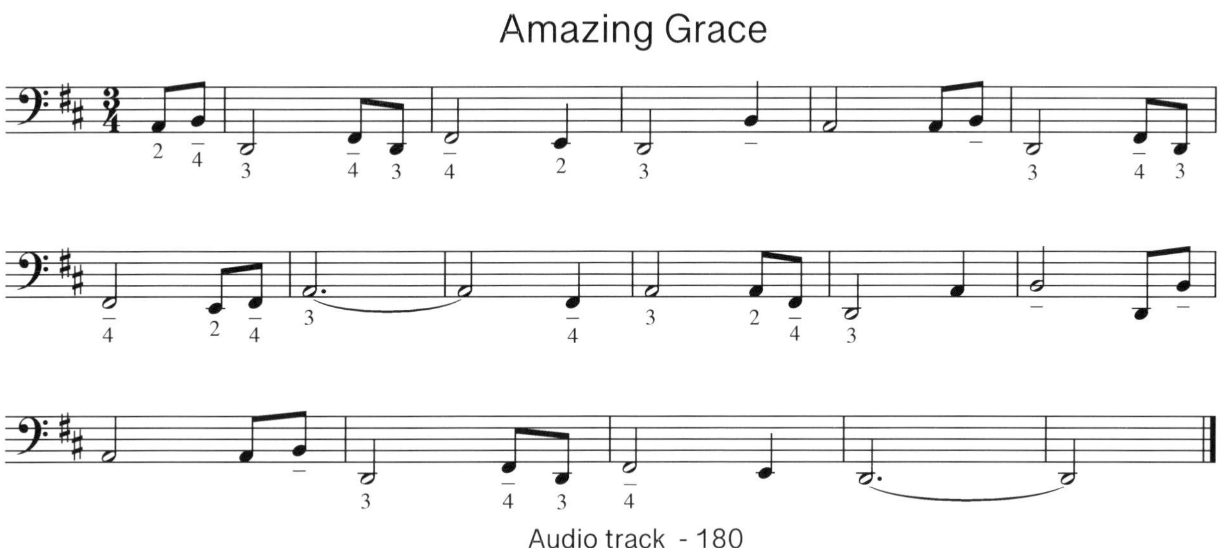

Audio track - 180

Come All Ye Fair and Tender Ladies

Audio track - 181

Simple Gifts

Audio track - 182

Exercises 7.7 and 7.8 introduce the F major scale. Notice the difference in note notation between the two exercises, though the fingering and bass buttons are the same. The B♭ bass button is below F, and D is its counter bass.

Exercise 7.7 - Audio track 54

Exercise 7.8 - Audio track 55

The time signature of Exercise 7.9 is 6/8, indicating there are six counts to each measure, with each eighth note getting one count. Use the standard major scale fingering throughout, except in measure 4 as indicated.

Exercise 7.9 - Audio track 56

In Exercise 7.10, ♫ = ♩♪ (triplet) indicates that eighth notes are to be played syncopated (see Syncopated Eighth Notes, page 10). Notice that measures 1 and 2 start with the third finger and use the same basic fingerings, though playing different notes. Keep your hand in the same shape as you move between these measures. Notice that there are other measures in this exercise that are also based on this same shape.

The E♭ in measure 4 is located below the B♭. The G in measure 2 and elsewhere is the counter bass of E♭. Notice that the G in measure 9 is not a counter bass.

Exercise 7.10 - Audio track 57

Even though Exercise 7.11 is in the key of F major, notice the D in measure 2 is not played as the counter bass of B♭. In measure 8, what is the enharmonic equivalent of G♭? (See Enharmonic Equivalents, page 9.) Answer: F♯ counter bass of D. In the final measure, the fifth finger is used. Does that finger feel weak? The next chapter includes exercises to develop its strength and agility.

Exercise 7.11 - Audio track 58

Exercise 7.12 has challenges. Be sure to use the correct fingering.

Exercise 7.12 - Audio track 59

Chapter 7 ends with three songs.

Jimmy Allen

Audio track - 183

The Star-Spangled Banner

Music Composed by
John Stafford Smith

Audio track - 184

Redwing

Audio track - 185

Chapter 8

Fifth Finger Workout

Exercises 8.1 through 8.10 emphasize use of the fifth finger, which typically is weaker and has less dexterity. Practice these exercises regularly and repeatedly to gain the necessary strength and agility to use the fifth finger as reliably as the others.

Repeat Exercise 8.1 numerous times, playing the notes staccato, non-legato, and legato.

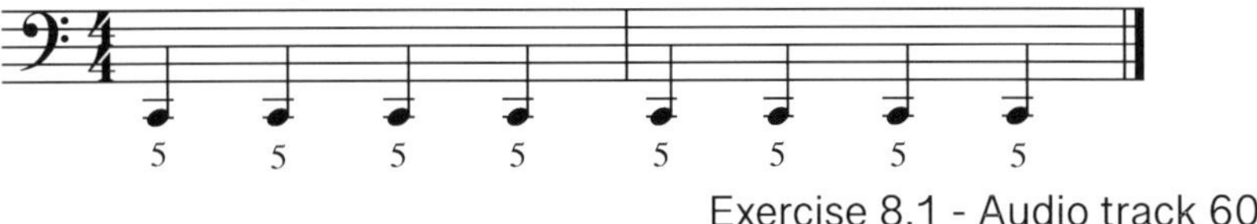

Exercise 8.1 - Audio track 60

In Exercise 8.2, the fifth finger works in combination with the other fingers.

Exercise 8.2 - Audio track 61

Pay attention to the fingerings in Exercise 8.3. Striking two consecutive notes with the fifth finger may feel awkward at first.

Exercise 8.3 - Audio track 62

In Exercise 8.4, pay attention to the fingering and counter bass indications.

Exercise 8.4 - Audio track 63

Exercise 8.5 is a series of repeating finger patterns. Use the indicated fingerings.

Exercise 8.5 - Audio track 64

Repeat the same finger pattern in each measure of Exercise 8.6.

Exercise 8.6 - Audio track 65

Repeat the same finger pattern in each measure of Exercise 8.7.

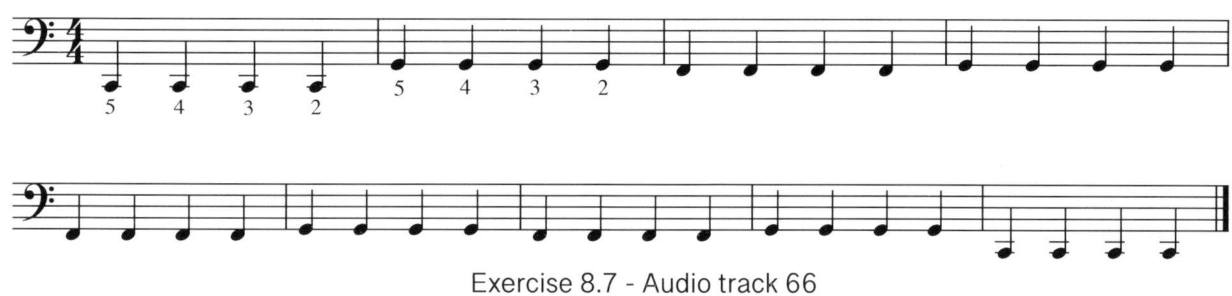

Exercise 8.7 - Audio track 66

Every measure in Exercise 8.8 uses the same repeating note pattern to create a C major scale ascending and descending.

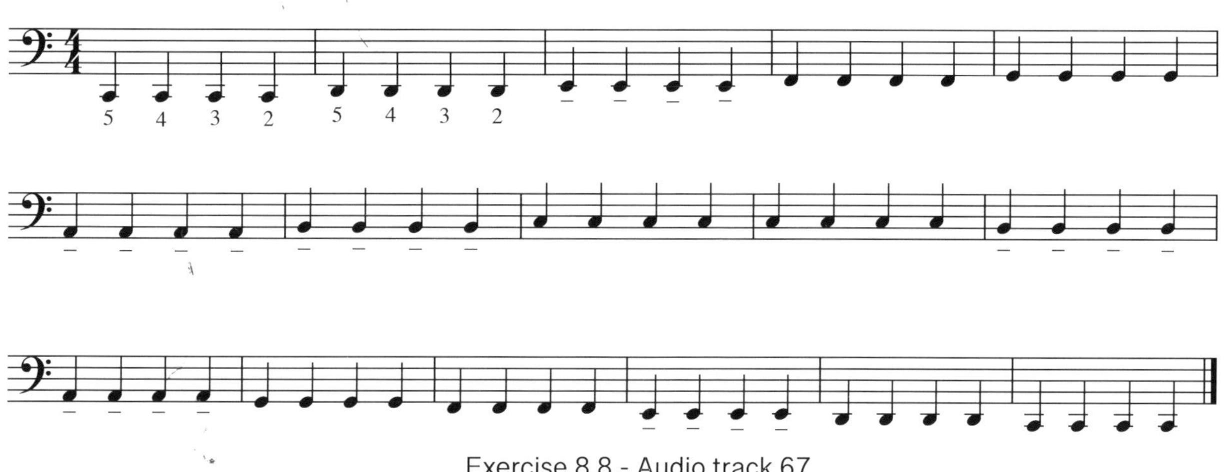

Exercise 8.8 - Audio track 67

Exercise 8.9 is in C Dorian mode which has a key signature of B♭ and E♭ and a tonal center of C. Be sure to use the indicated fingerings and counter basses.

Exercise 8.9 - Audio track 68

Exercise 8.10 is another boogie blues. The eighth notes are syncopated, as indicated by ♫ = ♩♪ (triplet). The note and fingering patterns of the first two measures (and their variations) repeat, sometime starting again on G, but sometimes on the notes C or D. Always start the pattern with the third finger as indicated.

Exercise 8.10 - Audio track 69

Section 2 finishes with five songs, all using the fifth finger where appropriate. Pay attention to fingering and counter bass indications.

Nonesuch

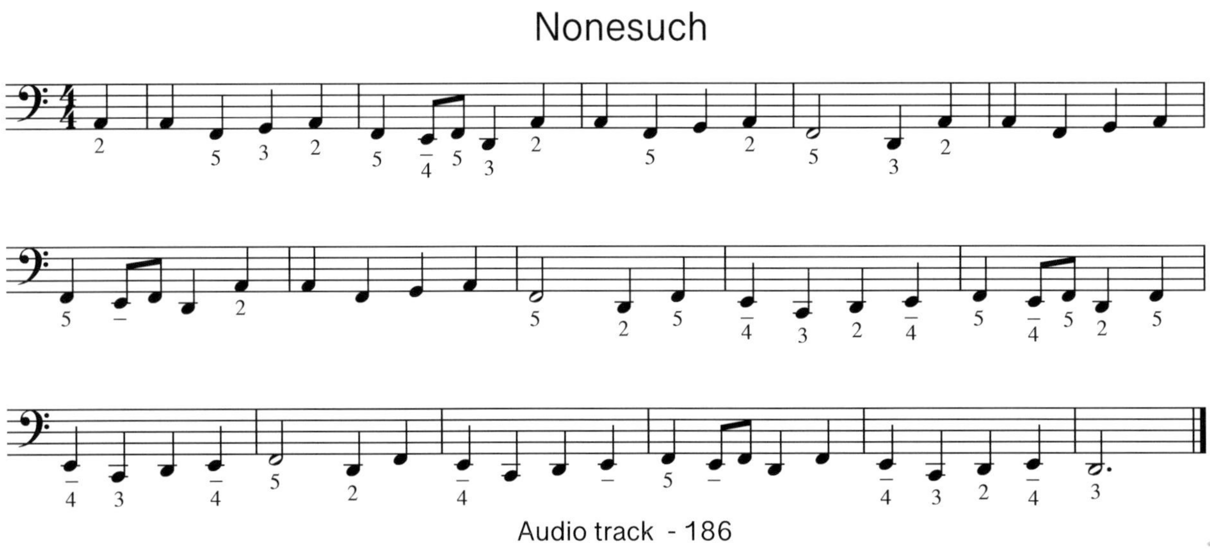

Audio track - 186

* G# is the counter bass of E.

On the Hills of Manchuria

Ilya Shatrov

* D# is the enharmonic equivalent of E♭ below B♭.

** G# is the enharmonic equivalent of A♭ below E♭.

Audio track - 189

Für Elise

Ludwig van Beethoven

* D# is the counter bass of B, above E.

Audio track - 190

Section 3
Chord Progressions

This section explores numerous common chord progressions with a focus on using chord tones, melodic passages, and walking bass lines to connect chords within the harmonic structure. The exercises also incorporate a variety of rhythmic patterns.

Chapter 9

Single Chord Patterns

We start with a review of bass note patterns available within a single chord. Exercise 9.1 is a simple alternating bass pattern.

Exercise 9.1 - Audio track 70

Exercise 9.2 is a pattern using the counter bass.

Exercise 9.2 - Audio track 71

Exercises 9.3 through 9.6 use both alternating and counter basses in various configurations.

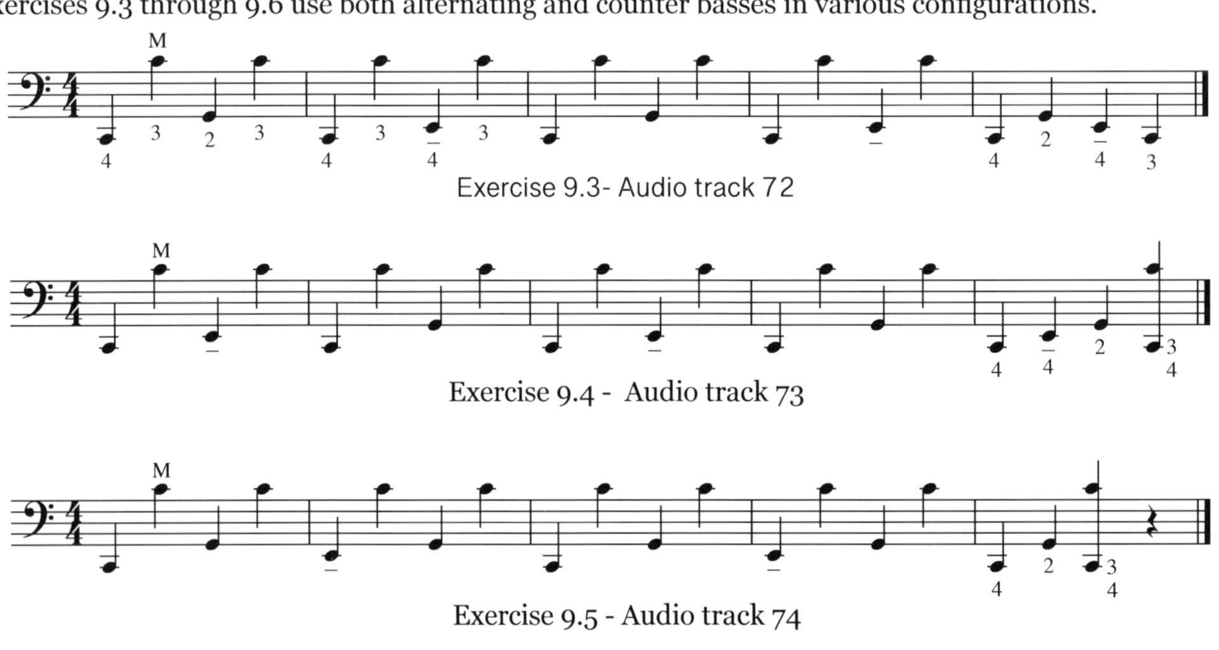

Exercise 9.3- Audio track 72

Exercise 9.4 - Audio track 73

Exercise 9.5 - Audio track 74

Exercise 9.6 - Audio track 75

Exercise 9.7 adds the note A, the sixth degree of the C chord into the pattern.

Exercise 9.7 - Audio track 76

Exercise 9.8 is another pattern incorporating the sixth of the chord.

Exercise 9.8 - Audio track 77

Exercise 9.9 uses both the 6th and ♭7th chord degrees, in this case the notes A and B♭. This is a typical boogie blues style accompaniment pattern. Chapter 18 includes many blues patterns similar to this.

Exercise 9.9 - Audio track 78

Exercise 9.10 is a simple alternating bass pattern in 3/4 time.

Exercise 9.10 - Audio track 79

Exercise 9.11 uses the counter bass in 3/4 time.

Exercise 9.11 - Audio track 80

Exercises 9.12 through 9.16 are based on Exercises 9.7 through 9.9. Exercise 9.12 is the same as Exercise 9.7, but the rhythm is syncopated. Syncopation can be indicated with the symbol ♫ = ♩♪ as seen in Exercise 9.12, or the timing can be explicitly notated as in Exercises 9.14 through 9.16. See Syncopated Eighth Notes (page 10) for a discussion about syncopation.

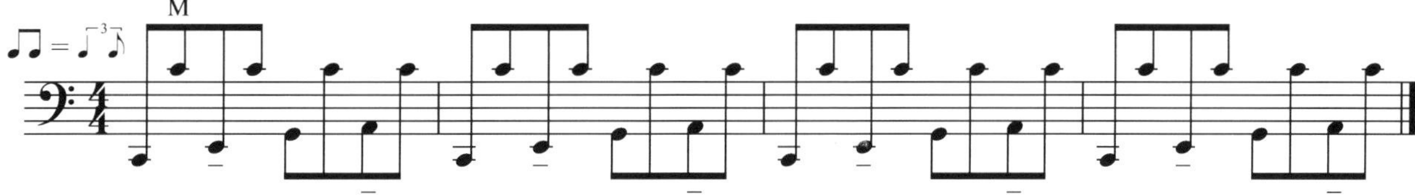

Exercise 9.12 - Audio track 81

Exercise 9.13 uses the seventh chord with a syncopated pattern.

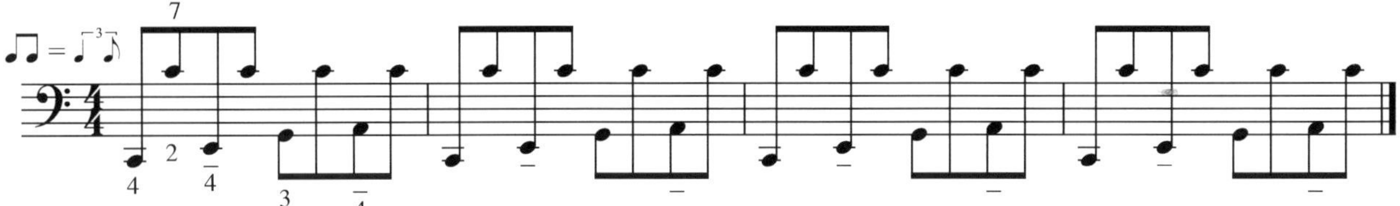

Exercise 9.13 - Audio track 82

Exercise 9.14 is similar to Exercise 9.8, but is syncopated.

Exercise 9.14 - Audio track 83

Exercise 9.15 is the same blues pattern as Exercise 9.9 but again, is syncopated.

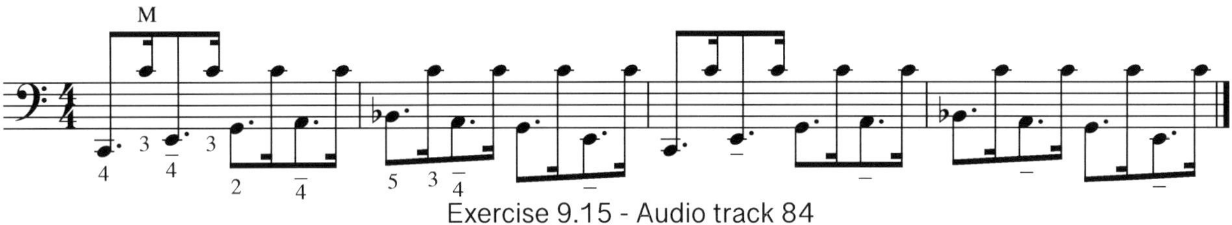

Exercise 9.15 - Audio track 84

Exercise 9.16 uses the seventh chord with the boogie pattern.

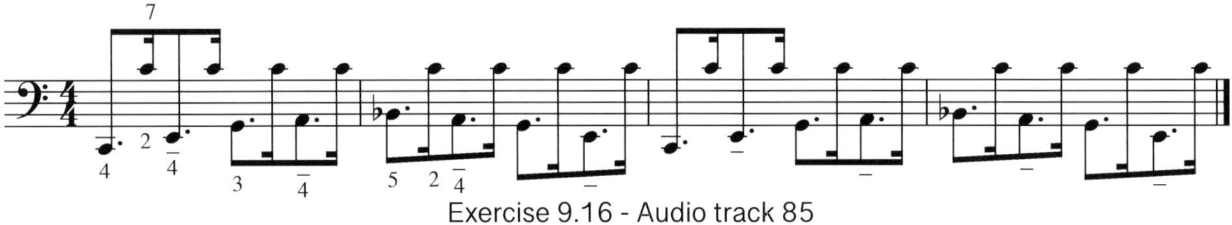

Exercise 9.16 - Audio track 85

Exercise 9.17 has a four note descending bass line within the chord.

Exercise 9.17 - Audio track 86

Exercise 9.18 uses the same notes as the above exercise, but in a different order.

Exercise 9.18 - Audio track 87

Exercise 9.19 uses a four note descending bass line, but with a ♭7.

Exercise 9.19 - Audio track 88

Exercise 9.20 uses the same notes as the above exercise, but with the seventh chord.

Exercise 9.20 - Audio track 89

Exercise 9.21 is a new pattern, adding the notes F and F♯.

Exercise 9.21 - Audio track 90

Exercise 9.22 uses the same notes as the above exercise, but is syncopated.

Exercise 9.22 - Audio track 91

Exercise 9.23 is an alternating bass pattern with the minor chord.

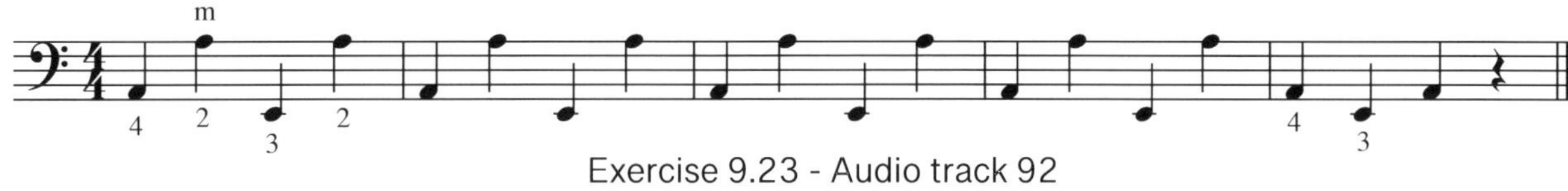

Exercise 9.23 - Audio track 92

Exercise 9.24 uses the minor third of the chord in the bass pattern. If you practiced the exercises in chapter eight, the fifth finger stretch should feel easy.

Exercise 9.24 - Audio track 93

Exercises 9.25 and 9.26 use both the alternating bass and the minor third in various configurations.

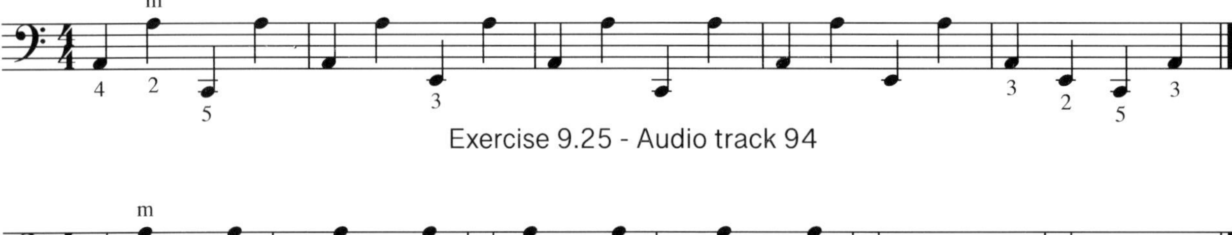

Exercise 9.25 - Audio track 94

Exercise 9.26 - Audio track 95

Exercise 9.27 uses a four note descending bass line with the minor chord. G♭ is the enharmonic equivalent of F♯, the counter bass of D. G♯ is the counter bass of E.

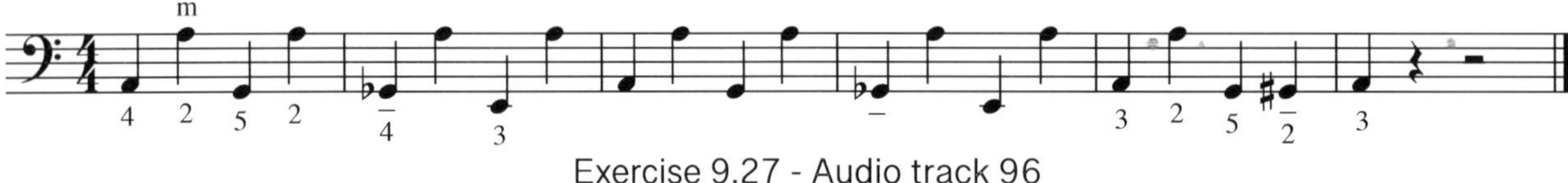

Exercise 9.27 - Audio track 96

Exercise 9.28 uses a different descending bass line from the above exercise.

Exercise 9.28 - Audio track 97

Exercise 9.29 uses a chromatic descending and ascending bass line. What is the enharmonic equivalent of A♭?

Exercise 9.29 - Audio track 98

Exercise 9.30 has a four note chromatic bass line. Notice that the chord pattern starts with the third finger.

Exercise 9.30 - Audio track 99

Exercise 9.31 uses a six note descending bass line with the minor chord.

Exercise 9.31 - Audio track 100

Chapter 10

The V - I and ii - V- I Chord Progressions

We will start with the two-chord progression from G7 to C major. This progression is often referred to as a perfect or authentic cadence. It is typically used to end a musical phrase or section, as it imparts a sense of finality. It is a basic building block of western harmony. We will explore this chord change first.

In Roman numeral terminology (see Chord Numbering, page 9), this progression is notated as V7 - I. The advantage of this nomenclature is that it is independent of the key signature. Thus, the harmonic function of the V7 - I progression is the same, no matter which key it is played in. G7 - C sounds the same harmonically as a D7 - G; it is just in a different key.

Exercises 10.1 through 10.5 show various note patterns and melodic lines which can be played between the G7 and C chords. Notice that the harmonic function of the G7 is to lead to the C major chord.

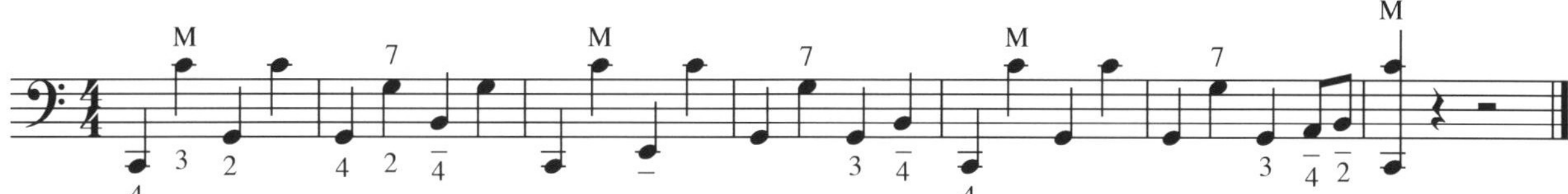

Exercise 10.1 - Audio track 101

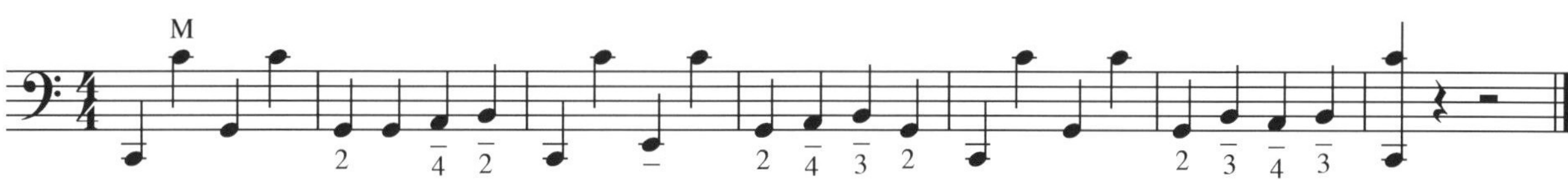

Exercise 10.2 - Audio track 102

In Exercise 10.3, A♯ is the same note as B♭, its enharmonic equivalent.

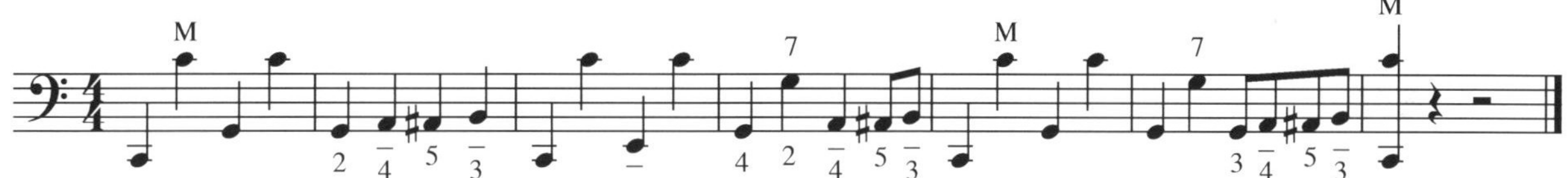

Exercise 10.3 - Audio track 103

Exercise 10.4 - Audio track 104

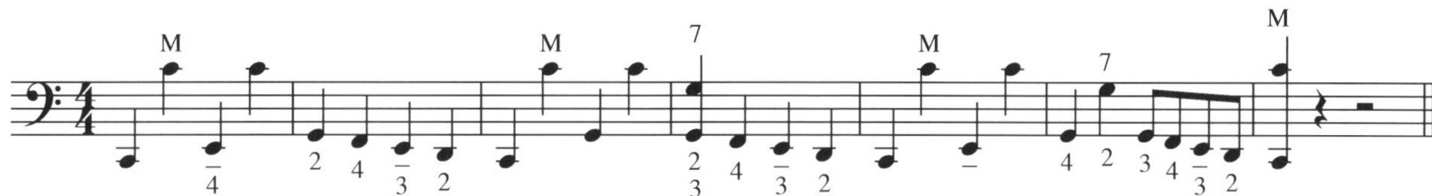

Exercise 10.5 - Audio track 105

The ii - V - I Chord Progression

ii - V - I is a commonly used chord progressions. It is considered one of the "strongest" progressions as it reinforces the key or tonal center of a phrase or piece of music. This progression is found in many musical genres, especially jazz.

Examples include:
Honey Suckle Rose by Fats Waller
Afternoon in Paris by John Lewis
Do You Want to Know a Secret? by The Beatles (composed by John Lennon and Paul McCartney)
Sunday Morning by Maroon 5

In the key of C major, the chords of a ii - V7 - I progression are Dm - G7 - C. See Illustration 10.1.

Illustration 10.1

Exercise 10.6 uses the ii - V7 - I progression with alternate and counter basses.

Exercise 10.6 - Audio track 106

Exercises 10.7 and 10.8 use chord tones to connect chords.

Exercise 10.7 - Audio track 107

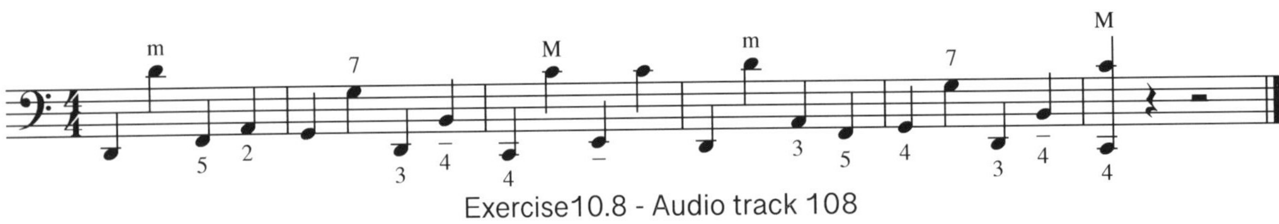

Exercise10.8 - Audio track 108

Exercise 10.9 uses chord and scale tones to approach the target note in ascending motion. See Connecting Chords (following page).

Exercise 10.9 - Audio track 109

Connecting Chords

All chords are not created equal. Within a song, some chords are stable and feel like home, some chords are unstable, leaving that home, while others are arriving home. Chord progression theory is beyond the scope of this book, though the study of it is highly recommended.

To create a smooth transition between chords, melodic or "walking" passages are employed. The starting place of a walking bass line is typically the root of the first chord, with the destination or "target" being the root of the following chord. The best note choices include chord tones and arpeggios, ascending or descending scale tones, half step chromatic movement, or some combination of all.

The last note before the destination chord is called the leading tone. The best leading tone choices include notes one half step below or above the root, a whole step below or above the root, or a perfect fifth above the root. For a G7 - C progression, these leading tone choices are B, D♭, A♯ (B♭), D, and G respectively.

Exercise 10.10 shows a walking bass line. Notice the same note pattern is repeated but with different bass buttons and fingerings. Though the chords are absent, the note choices imply the ii - V - I progression.

Exercise 10.10 - Audio track 110

Exercise 10.11 uses ascending chromatic lines to approach the target notes (see Connecting Chords above). What is the enharmonic equivalent of A♯?

Exercise 10.11 - Audio track 111

Exercise 10.12 shows an ascending bass line with scale and chromatic tones. Notice the same note pattern is repeated using different bass buttons.

Exercise 10.12 - Audio track 112

Exercise 10.13 uses descending lines to approach the target note.

Exercise 10.13- Audio track 113

Exercise 10.14 uses a descending walking bass line. The line is repeated, with chords added.

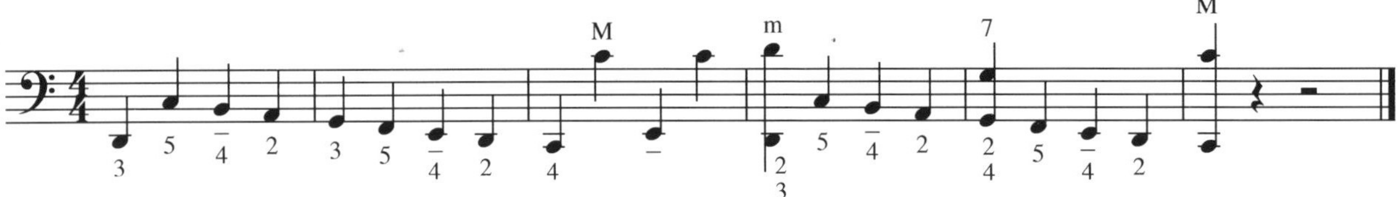

Exercise 10.14 - Audio track 114

Exercise 10.15 uses descending lines with chromatic movement. What are the enharmonic equivalents of A♭ and D♭?

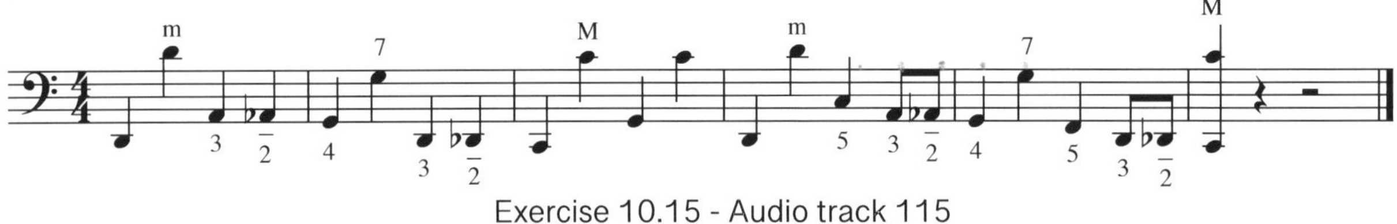

Exercise 10.15 - Audio track 115

Exercise 10.16 uses chromatic patterns to reach the target chords.

Exercise 10.16 - Audio track 116

Exercise 10.17 shows a descending bass line with scale and chromatic tones.

Exercise 10.17 - Audio track 117

Exercise 10.18 uses mostly chord tones between chords, but includes some chromatic movement as well. What is the enharmonic of A♯?

Exercise 10.18 - Audio track 118

As indicated, play Exercise 10.19 with syncopated eighth notes.

Exercise 10.19 - Audio track 119

Exercise 10.20 explores the ii -V- I change in the key of G major.

Exercise 10.20 - Audio track 120

Exercise 10.21 explores the ii -V- I change in the key of F major. Chords, scales, and chromatic tones are used. Pay attention to enharmonics. The A♭ in measure 8 is below the E♭ bass button. Play with syncopation.

Exercise 10.21 - Audio track 121

Exercise 10.22 presents the ii -V- I change in the key of D major. The enharmonic of F♮ in the pickup measure and elsewhere is the E♯ counter bass of C♯, above the F♯ bass button. D# in measures 4 and 12 is the counter bass of B. B♭ in measure 9 is the enharmonic equivalent of the A♯ counter bass of F♯. What is the enharmonic equivalent of E♭ in measure 10?

Exercise 10.22 - Audio track 122

Chapter 11

The IV - V7 - I Chord Progression

As in the previous chapter, the IV - V7 - I progression is in the "most used" category. It is often referred to as the most important chord progression, because it contains the three main harmonic components of a key—the tonic (I chord), the dominant (V chord), and the subdominant (IV chord).

There are literally thousands of songs which use these chords as their foundation. It is commonly heard in folk, rock, country, and blues genres among others.

Songs based on the I - IV - V7 chords include:
La Bamba adapted by Ritchie Valens
Mr. Tambourine Man by Bob Dylan
Twist And Shout by The Beatles (composed by Phil Medley and Bert Russell)
Life Likes Poetry by Merle Haggard

In the key of C major, the chords of a IV -V7- I progression are F - G7 - C. See Illustration 11.1.

Illustration 11.1

Exercise 11.1 uses the IV - V7 - I progression mainly with chord tones.

Exercise 11.1 - Audio track 123

Exercise 11.2 uses scale tones between chords. Notice when counter basses are and are not used.

Exercise 11.2 - Audio track 124

Exercise 11.3 explores the IV - V7 - I change in the key of G major.

Exercise 11.3 - Audio track 125

Exercise 11.4 uses bass lines with scale and chromatic tones. Pay attention to enharmonic equivalents.

Exercise 11.4 - Audio track 126

Exercise 11.5 uses both the IV - V7 - I and the ii -V- I chord progressions in the key of F major.

Exercise 11.5 - Audio track 127

Chapter 12

The I - vi - IV - V7 and I - vi - ii - V7 Chord Progressions

The I - vi - IV - V7 progression is sometimes called the doo-wop progression, as the chord cycle was often used in doo-wop music, a genre that was popular in America starting in the 1940s and continuing through the early 1960s. The I - vi - ii - V is a variation, substituting the related and darker ii chord for the brighter IV chord.

Songs using the I - vi - IV - V progression include:
Last Kiss by Wayne Cochran
I Will Always Love You by Dolly Parton
Every Breath You Take by Sting
D'yer Mak'er by Led Zeppelin

Songs using the I - vi - ii - V progression include:
Blue Moon by Richard Rodgers and Lorenz Hart
Don't Look Back by John Lee Hooker
Hungry Heart by Bruce Springsteen
Die In Your Arms by Justin Bieber

In the key of C major, the chords of this progression are C - Am - F (or Dm) - G7. See Illustration 12.1.

Illustration 12.1

Exercise 12.1 explores the I - vi - IV - V progression with chords tones and walking bass lines.

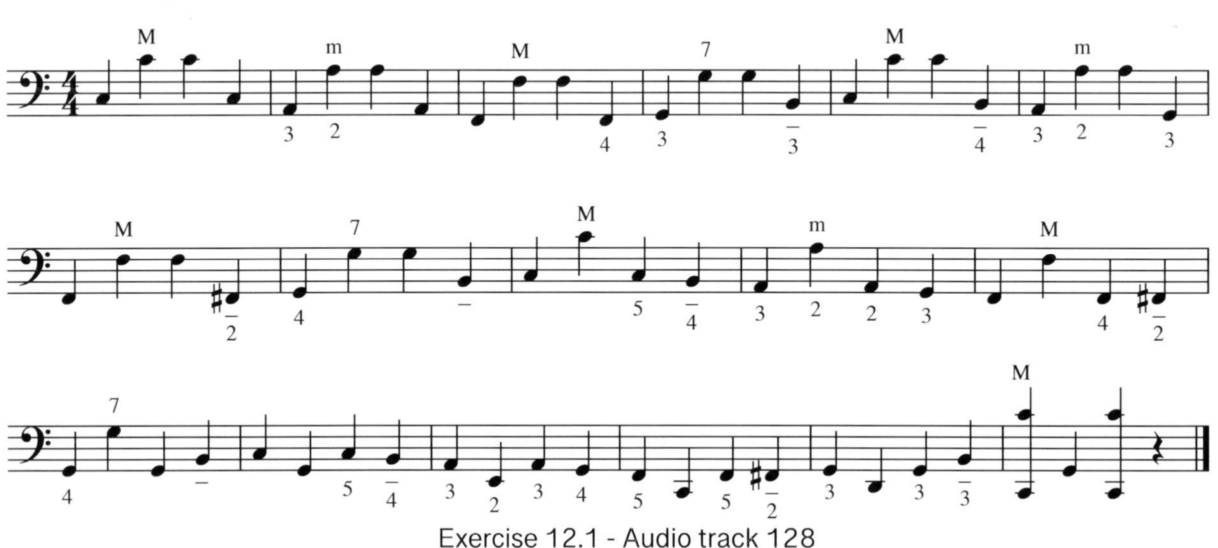

Exercise 12.1 - Audio track 128

Exercise 12.2 is in the key of G major. The 6/8 time signature was frequently used in doo-wop songs. What is the enharmonic of D♭?

Exercise 12.2 - Audio track 129

Exercise 12.3 uses the I - vi - IV - V progression with chords and walking bass lines. Pay attention to enharmonics and counter bass indications. A♭ in measure 15 is below the E♭ bass button.

Exercise 12.3 - Audio track 130

Exercise 12.4 uses the I - vi - ii - V progression with chords and walking bass lines. The latter half of the exercise may be a challenge for your fifth finger.

Exercise 12.4 - Audio track 131

In Exercise 12.5 pay attention to enharmonics and counter bass indications.

Exercise 12.5 - Audio track 132

Chapter 13

The I - V - vi - IV Progression and Variations

The I - V - vi - IV progression and its variations are favored in contemporary pop, rock, and country music in part due to the emotional character inherent in the chord cycle.

Songs using this progression include:
Don't Stop Believin' by Journey (composed by Steve Perry, Jonathan Cain, Neal Schon)
All Too Well by Taylor Swift
Hair by Lady Gaga (composed by Lady Gaga and Nadir Khayat)
I'm Going Down by Bruce Springsteen

In the key of C major, the progression's chords are C - G - Am - F. See Illustration 13.1.

Illustration 13.1

Exercise 13.1 explores the I - V - vi - IV progression with chords and walking bass lines.

Exercise 13.1 - Audio track 133

Exercise 13.2 is in the key of G major with a rhythm based on the dotted quarter-note beginning each measure.

Exercise 13.2 - Audio track 134

Be sure to play the correct rhythm in Exercise 13.3. In measure 11, F♯ is above the B bass button.

Exercise 13.3 - Audio track 135

Exercise 13.4 starts the chord cycle on the vi chord, which in the key of F major is Dm.

Exercise 13.4 - Audio track 136

I - V - ♭VII - IV is a variation of the I - V - vi - IV progression. In the key of C major, the chords are C - G - B♭ - F, as shown in Illustration 13.2.

Illustration 13.2

Exercise 13.5 uses the I - V - ♭VII - IV progression. It can be played with straight or syncopated eighth notes. What is the enharmonic equivalent of G♯?

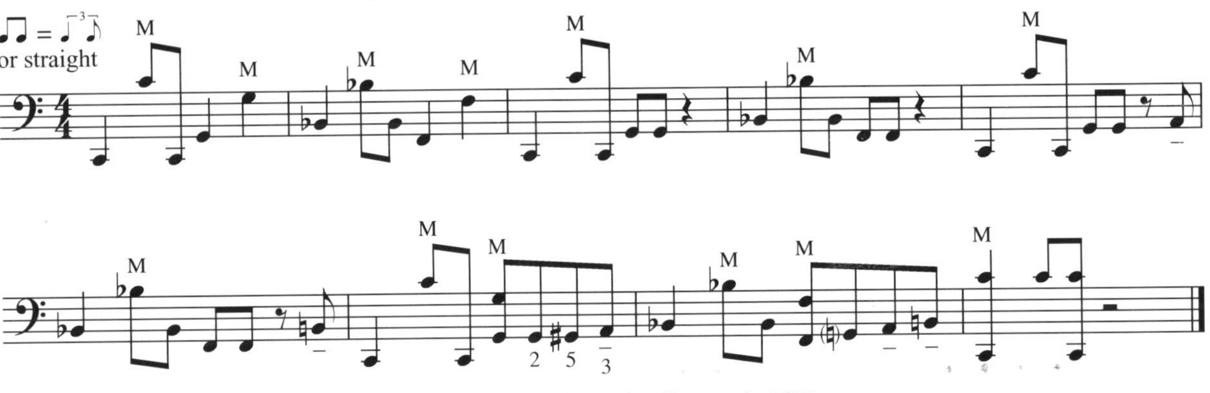

Exercise 13.5 - Audio track 137

Exercise 13.6 is in G Mixolydian mode, with a tonal center of G and a key signature of no sharps and no flats. Notice the enharmonics.

Exercise 13.6 - Audio track 138

Chapter 14

The Canon Progression I – V – vi – iii – IV – I – IV – V

It is not precisely known when Johann Pachelbel composed his Canon and Gigue for 3 Violins and Basso Continuo (also known as Canon and Gigue in D). The composition was not published or performed until a 1968 recording by French conductor Jean-François Paillard, when the piece's path to popularity began. The chord cycle is now known as Pachelbel's Canon Progression and can be heard in many contemporary songs, including:

Go West by The Village People (composed by Henri Belolo, Victor Willis, Jacques Morali)
Get Me Away From Here, I'm Dying by Belle and Sebastian (composed by Stuart Murdoch)
Graduation (Friends Forever) by Vitamin C (composed by Vitamin C and Josh Deutsch)
Let It Be by The Beatles (composed by John Lennon and Paul McCartney)

In the key of C major, the progression's chords are C - G - Am - Em - F - C - F - G. See Illustration 14.1.

Illustration 14.1

Exercise 14.1 explores the progression with basic chord formations. Moving accurately from Em to F may be a challenge at first.

Exercise 14.1 - Audio track 139

Exercise 14.2 is in the key of F major and uses the chord progression with chord tones and walking bass lines.

Exercise 14.2 - Audio track 140

Chapter 15

The Andalusian Cadence i – ♭VII – ♭VI – V

This descending chord pattern is quite common in Flamenco music. Andalusia, the birthplace of the guitar-centric style, is in southern Spain. The progression is now found in many genres, including classical music, rock, and jazz.

Songs using this progression include:
Hit the Road Jack by Ray Charles (composed by Percy Mayfield)
Good Vibrations by The Beach Boys (composed by Brian Wilson)
Sultans of Swing by Dire Straits (composed by Mark Knopfler)
Babe I'm Gonna Leave You by Led Zeppelin (composed by Robert Plant)

In the key of Am, the chords of this progression are Am - G - F - E. See Illustration 15.1.

Illustration 15.1

The chord cycle can also be played with dominant seven chords. See Illustration 15.2.

Illustration 15.2

Exercise 15.1 uses the progression with basic chord formations and passing chord tones.

Exercise 15.1 - Audio track 141

Exercise 15.2 is in the key of D minor, and is based on the rhythm ♩. ♩. ♩

Exercise 15.2 - Audio track 142

Exercise 15.3 uses the progression with chord tones and walking bass lines. Notice the enharmonics. F♮ in measure 16 is the enharmonic of E♯, counter bass of C♯.

Exercise 15.3 - Audio track 143

Chapter 16

The Minor ii – V – i Chord Progression

Minor ii - V - i is a commonly used progression in jazz. Since jazz chords typically include the seventh scale degree, we will review how to play seventh and other extended chord formations on the accordion's bass, before the chapter's exercises.

In the key of C minor, the ii - V - i progression is Dm - G - Cm. We can easily add the seventh to the G chord to play Dm - G7 - Cm. See Illustration 16.1.

Illustration 16.1

In the key of C minor, the C harmonic minor scale (Illustration 16.2) is typically used to build chords. Notice the scale includes E♭, A♭, and B♮. How do these notes affect the chords of this progression?

Illustration 16.2

The iim7(♭5) Chord

The notes of the D minor chord are D, F, and A. Notice that the sixth degree of the C harmonic minor scale is A♭, not A. If using only the harmonic minor scale tones, the notes of the ii chord are D, F, and A♭, which is called Dm(♭5) or D diminished fifth. See Illustration 16.3.

Illustration 16.3

To add the seventh scale degree, the note C is included. This chord is called a m7(♭5) or half-diminished. Illustration 16.4 shows the Dm7(♭5) with the notes D, F, A♭, and C. Notice the half-diminished symbol. m7(♭5) and ø both refer to the same chord.

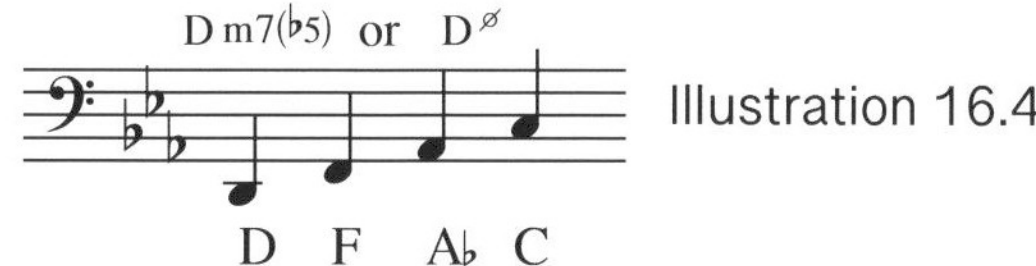

Illustration 16.4

How does the half-diminished compare to the diminished chord? The notes of D diminished are D, F, Ab, and B♮ (Illustration 16.5). On most modern accordions, the diminished button plays three, not four notes. The ♭5 is typically omitted. Consequently the D diminished button sounds the notes D, F, and B♮, omitting the A♭.

Illustration 16.5

The m7(♭5) chord can be played on the accordion's bass side. Notice that the upper three notes of the Dm7(♭5) are F, A♭, and C, which is F minor. The combination of D bass played with a F minor chord creates a Dm7(♭5). Illustration 16.6 shows how this combination is notated for the accordion. Notice there are three possible fingering combinations: D bass button played with the second finger and Fm with the fourth finger, fingers three and five play these same buttons, or D counter bass played with the fourth finger and Fm with the second.

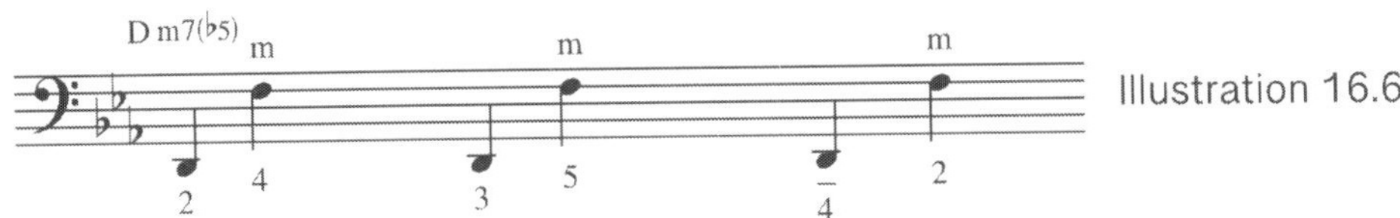

Illustration 16.6

The V7(♭9) Chord

In jazz, the ♭9 is often added to the V7 to create a V7(♭9) chord when playing a minor ii - V - i progression. The notes of the G7 chord are G, B, D, and F. The notes of a G7♭9 chord are G, B, D, F, and A♭. See Illustration 16.7.

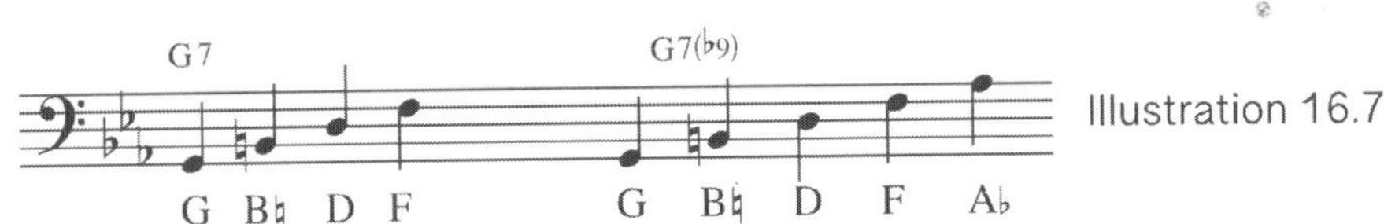

Illustration 16.7

Can a V7(♭9) chord be played on the accordion's bass side? Notice the top three notes of the G7♭9 are D, F, and A♭. These are the same notes played by the F diminished button. Combining the G major chord with the F diminished chord creates the G7♭9. Illustration 16.8 shows how this is notated for the accordion. G bass is played with the fourth finger, F diminished is played with the second finger, and G major with the third finger. This shape will likely feel quite awkward at first but will become accessible with practice. Illustration 16.8 also shows an optional fingering omitting the G major (leaving the B♮ out of the chord).

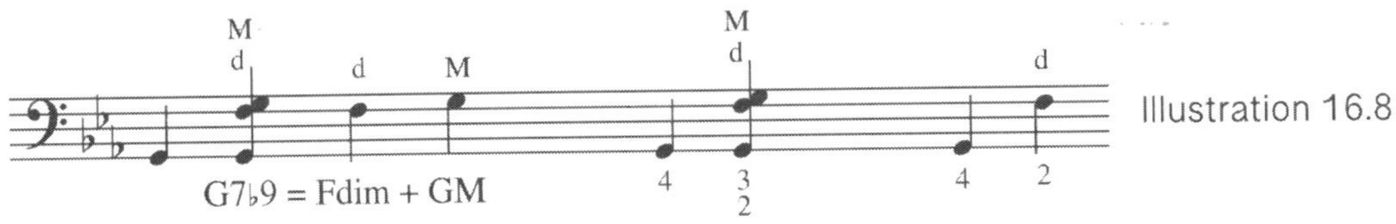

Illustration 16.8

The i Chord

In a ii - V - i progression, the i chord is often played as a m7 or m6. The notes of C minor are C, E♭, and G (Illustration 16.9). The notes of a Cm7 are C, E♭, G, and B♭ (Illustration 16.10). Notice the top three notes of the Cm7 are E♭, G, and B♭, which is E♭ Major. E♭M and Cm can be combined to play Cm7. Illustration 16.11 shows how this is notated for the accordion and the various fingering options for the bass button combinations. In the last option of Illustration 16.11, C is the counter bass of A♭.

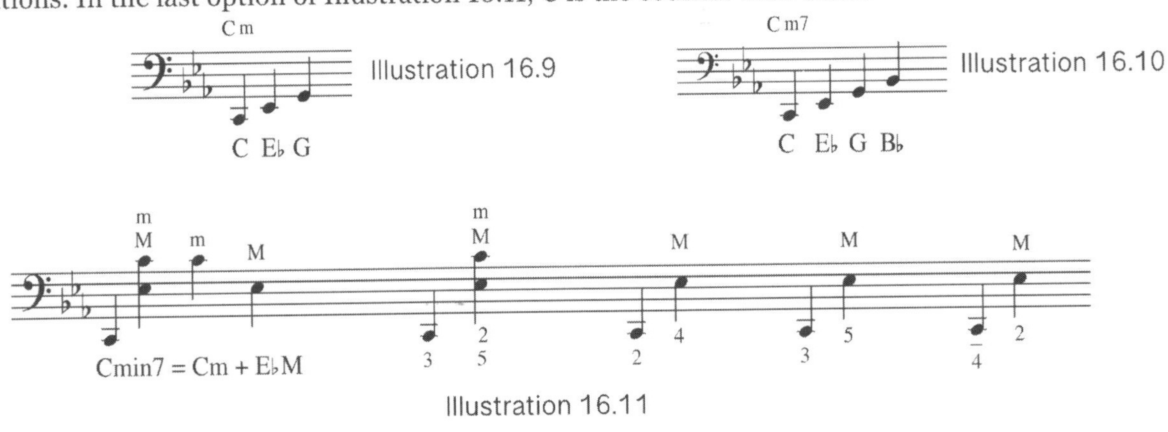

Illustration 16.9

Illustration 16.10

Illustration 16.11

The Cm6 chord is C, E♭, G, and A♮ (Illustration 16.12). The notes of the Cdim are C, E♭, G♭, and A♮ (Illustration 16.13). As mentioned above, most accordions do not play the ♭5 in the diminished chord. The Cdim button plays the notes C, E♭, and A. Without the G♭ in the diminished chord, the Cm and Cdim buttons can be combined to play a Cm6. Illustration 16.14 shows how this is notated and fingered.

Below are some examples of the ii - V - i chord progression in the key of A minor.

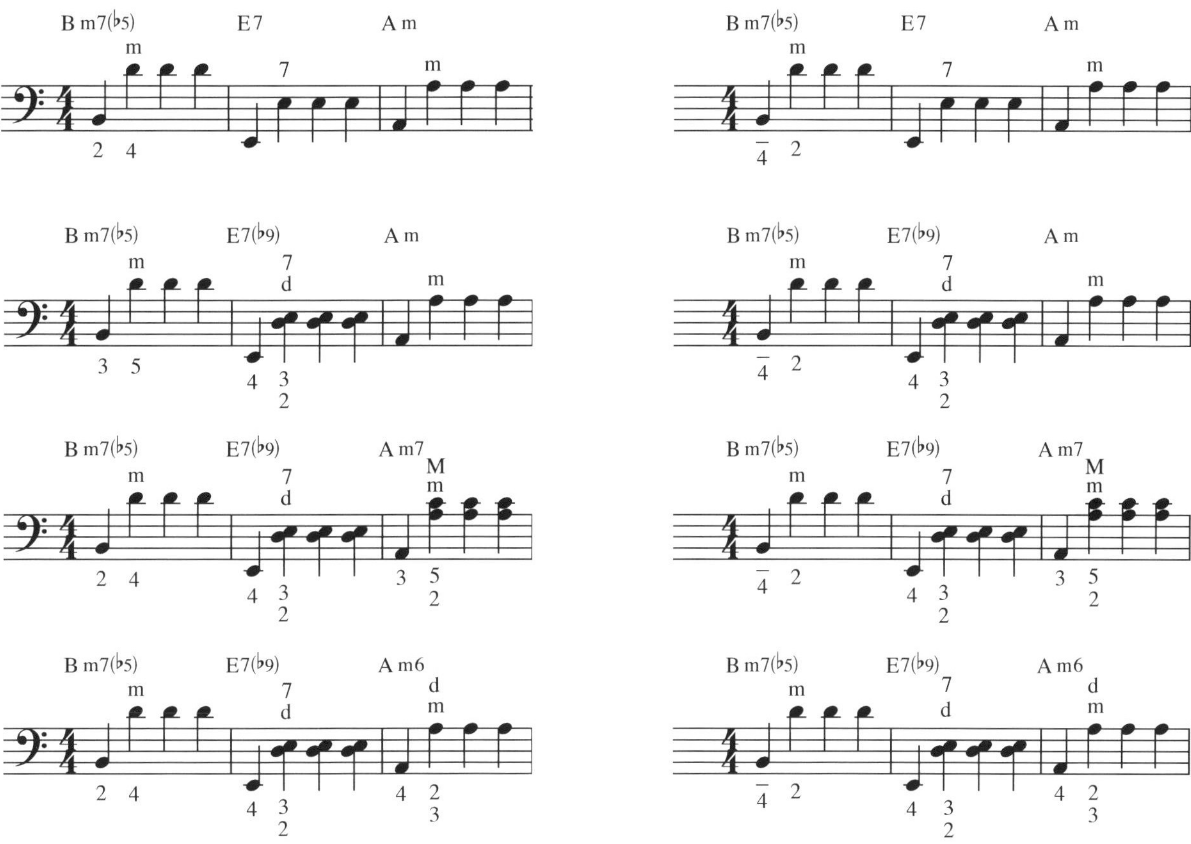

In Exercise 16.1, the Bm7(♭5) chord is played in various shapes.

Exercise 16.1 - Audio track 144

Exercise 16.2 uses the ii7(♭5) - V7 - i progression in the key of G minor. In measures 9 through 14, be sure to hold the bass notes down when indicated as whole or half notes.

Exercise 16.2 - Audio track 145

Exercise 16.3 has more bass note activity.

Exercise 16.3 - Audio track 146

Exercise 16.4 is in the key of C minor. It is played with syncopated eighth notes and incorporates walking bass lines. A♭ in measures 1, 5, and 13 is below the E♭ bass button.

Exercise 16.4 - Audio track 147

Exercise 16.5 is in the key of D minor. Notice the use of the Dm7 chord. B♭ in measure 1, 5, and 13 is the enharmonic of A♯, the counter bass of F♯.

Exercise 16.5 - Audio track 148

Exercise 16.6 focuses on the V7(♭9) chord. With practice, the button combination will feel less awkward.

Exercise 16.6 - Audio track 149

Exercise 16.7 includes both iim7 and V7(♭9) chords. Notice where chord buttons are subtracted or added within the same measure. Pay attention to counter bass indications.

Exercise 16.7 - Audio track 150

Exercise 16.8 is challenging, especially for the fifth finger. Notice the use of the im6 chord. What is the enharmonic equivalent of G♭? E♭ in measure 26 is the enharmonic of D♯, the counter bass of B.

Exercise 16.8 - Audio track 151

Chapter 17

And a Few More

This chapter presents a few additional chord progressions not in the "most popular" category, but are nonetheless worth exploring.

The I - IV - I - V Progression

In the key of C major the I - IV - I - V progression is C - F - C - G. Exercise 17.1 uses the progression with chord tones and walking bass lines.

Exercise 17.1 - Audio track 152

Exercise 17.2 is in the key of D major. Be sure to use the correct timing.

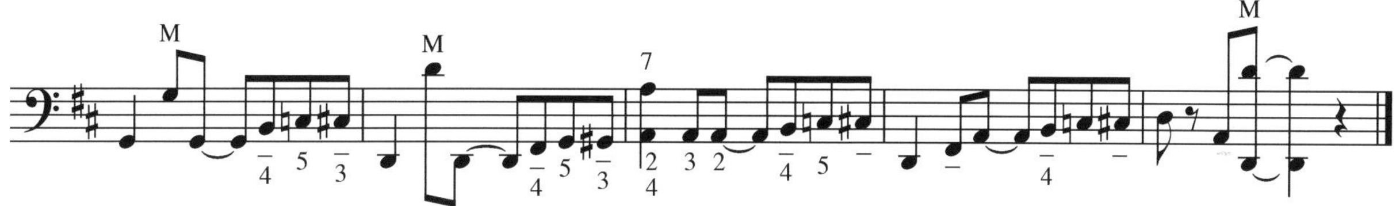

Exercise 17.2 - Audio track 153

The I - ii - IV - V Progression

In the key of C major, the chords of the I - ii - IV - V progression are C - Dm - F - G. Exercise 17.3 uses this progression and the variation I - IV - ii - V.

Exercise 17.3 - Audio track 154

Exercise 17.4 uses chord tones and walking bass lines to bridge the chord changes.

Exercise 17.4 - Audio track 155

The I - ii - iii - IV - V Progression

In the key of C major, the chords of a I - ii - iii - IV - V progression are C - Dm - Em - F - G, as used in exercise 17.5. Notice whether the note E is played with the bass or counter bass.

Exercise 17.5 - Audio track 156

Exercise 17.6 uses the progression in the key of G major. Bm in measure 3 and elsewhere is above Em. A# in measures 14 and 15 is the counter bass of F#, above B. D# in measures 21 and 22 is the counter bass of B.

Exercise 17.6 - Audio track 157

The i - iv - V Progression

The chords of the i - iv - V progression are Cm - Fm - G in the key of C minor. Exercise 17.7 explores the progression with chord tones and walking bass lines. In measure 20, hold the tied B♮ down for two counts while striking the G7 chord only on count 2.

Exercise 17.7 - Audio track 158

In Exercise 17.8, pay attention to enharmonics.

Exercise 17.8 - Audio track 159

In Exercise 17.9, syncopate the eighth notes.

Exercise 17.9 - Audio track 160

The i - III - iv - VI Progression

In the key of Em, the chords of the i - III - iv - VI progression are Em - G - Am - C, as shown in Exercise 17.10.

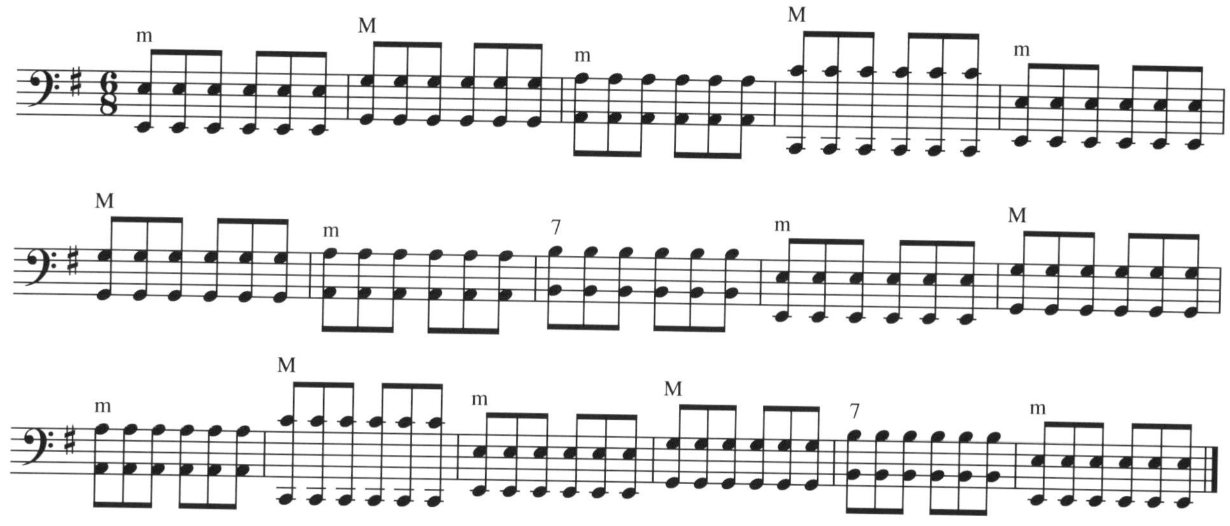

Exercise 17.10 - Audio track 161

In Exercise 17.11, the progression is played in the key of A minor.

Exercise 17.11 - Audio track 162

Chapter 18

12 Bar Blues

This chapter presents numerous bass patterns, or riffs, which are common to the blues. The exercises are limited to the standard 12 bar blues form. For a more detailed exploration of blues, check out the book *Learn Blues Accordion—A Comprehensive Guide to Mastering the Blues* (Mel Bay Publications MB30520M).

The basic 12 bar blues chord sequence is:

I7 | I7 | I7 | I7 |
IV7 | IV7 | I7 | I7 |
V7 | V7 | I7 | I7 |

In the key of G, the chords are:

G7 | G7 | G7 | G7 |
C7 | C7 | G7 | G7 |
D7 | D7 | G7 | G7 |

There are of course variations to this pattern, as we shall see.

The first three exercises are based on a blues style commonly called boogie-woogie. Illustration 18.1 shows two basic boogie patterns and their fingerings. These patterns, like most of the blues, are played with syncopated eighth notes (see Syncopated Eighth Notes, page 10).

Illustration 18.1

Exercise 18.1 uses the boogie-woogie in the common 12 bar blues form. Notice how the two patterns shown in Illustration 18.1 are juxtaposed and varied. There is no one "right" way to play the blues—improvisation is common in this genre. Remember to syncopate the eighth notes.

Exercise 18.1 - Audio track 163

In Exercise 18.2, walking bass lines are added into some of the chord changes. Notice the basic chord sequence is altered. In measure 2, the IV7 chord substitutes for the I7. In measure 10, the IV7 chord substitutes for the V7. A♯ in measure 4 is the enharmonic of B♭. D♭ in measure 9 is the enharmonic of C♯, the counter bass of A.

Exercise 18.2 - Audio track 164

Play Exercise 18.3 with a slow to moderate swing feel. The exercise is in the key of D and utilizes walking bass lines with lots of chromatic movement. Pay attention to enharmonics. The 12 bar sequence is played twice through. Notice the use of the A7 chord in measure 12, bridging the two 12 bar cycles.

Exercise 18.3 - Audio track 165

Illustration 18.2 shows the basic riff of the following exercise. Though no chord buttons are played, the harmonies are clearly implied by the bass notes.

Illustration 18.2

In Exercise 18.4, the shape (note pattern and fingering) of the riff is the same for each implied chord, with slight variations. Move your hand as you play from one chord position to the next but keep the shape. The pattern sounds good with either straight or syncopated eighths. What is the enharmonic of D♯?

Exercise 18.4 - Audio track 166

The riff of Exercise 18.5 incorporates triplets. The eighth notes within the triplet are not syncopated. The enharmonic equivalent of D♯ is E♭, A♯ is B♭, and G♯ is A♭.

Exercise 18.5 - Audio track 167

Illustration 18.3 shows the riff and a variation used in Exercise 18.6.

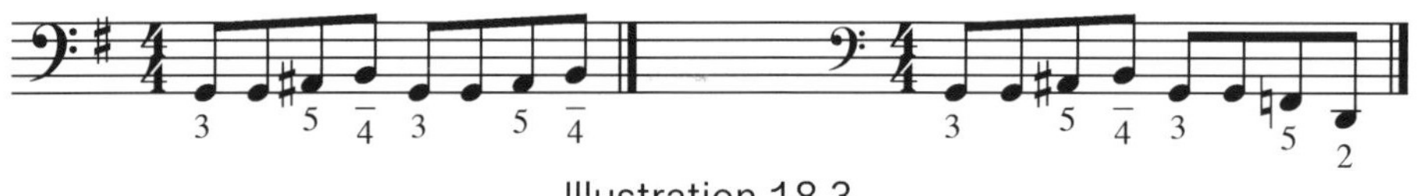

Illustration 18.3

Exercise 18.6 is played with straight eighths and provides a good workout for the fourth and fifth fingers.

Exercise 18.6 - Audio track 168

Illustration 18.4 introduces a blues rhythm commonly called the shuffle. The basic note pattern and a variation are shown. The counter bass indication refers to the E, played as the counter bass of C.

Illustration 18.4

Exercise 18.7 uses the shuffle with the basic blues chord sequence. Notice the note pattern and fingering is the same for all chords. Shift your hand when moving from one chord to another, maintaining the same shape.

Exercise 18.7 - Audio track 169

Exercise 18.8 uses the shuffle and its variation.

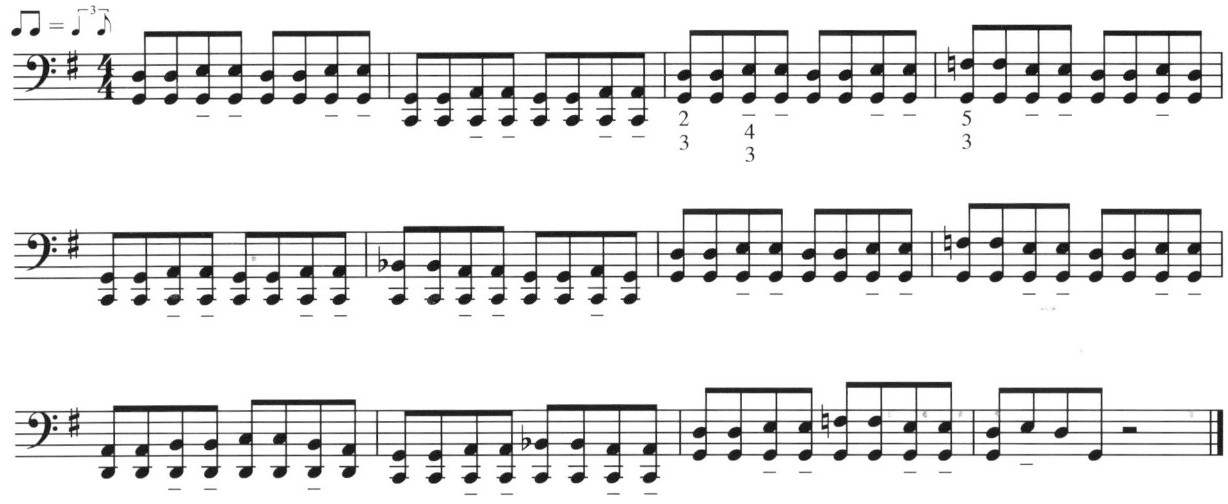

Exercise 18.8 - Audio track 170

Illustration 18.5 introduces another blues pattern.

Illustration 18.5

Exercise 18.9 is based on the above pattern. Pay attention to enharmonics.

Exercise 18.9 - Audio track 171

Exercise 18.10 uses a variation of the above pattern.

Exercise 18.10 - Audio track 172

Another blues riff is introduced in Illustration 18.6. Again, the eighth notes within the triplet are not syncopated.

Illustration 18.6

Exercise 18.11 uses the above riff and related variations. It also incorporates various blues riffs from previous exercises.

Exercise 18.11 - Audio track 173

Below are a few more blues riffs. With the knowledge you have gained from the exercises in this chapter, you now know how to use them. Remember, blues is improvisational. Have fun making up your own blues tunes.

This page intentionally left blank.

Mel Bay Presents

Accordion Books by David DiGiuseppe

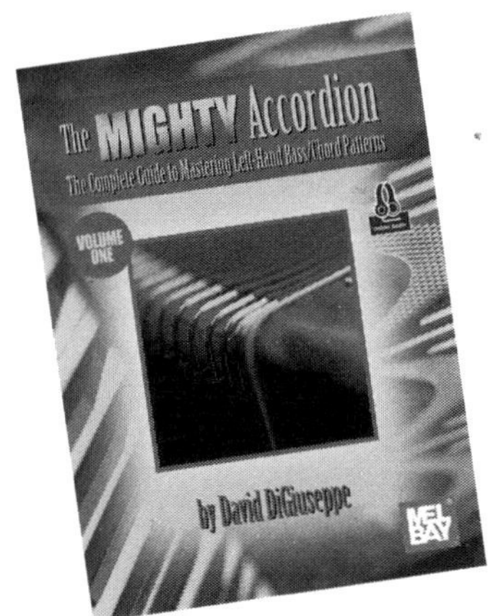

The Mighty Accordion Volume One

The Complete Guide to Mastering Left-Hand Bass/Chord Patterns

A truly unique and much-needed guide to playing the bass side of the accordion. A comprehensive collection of progressive exercises guide the student in learning and mastering bass/chord patterns. Beginning chapters assume little knowledge of the instrument and teach simple accompaniment patterns. For the intermediate player, exercises using the major, minor, seventh, and diminished chords are included. For the advanced player, latter chapters present exercises on chord combinations needed to play sixth, minor seventh, major seventh, ninth, and other advanced chords. Includes online audio.

Learn Blues Accordion

A Comprehensive Guide to Mastering the Blues

A comprehensive method book with 34 blues compositions and numerous exercises. The material starts easy and progresses in difficulty as new concepts and techniques are introduced including blues scales, chord progressions, grace notes, slides, pedal points, double stops, and tremolos. Left-hand rhythmic styles are explained and used throughout the book, including boogie-woogie, the shuffle, New Orleans' second line, and walking bass lines. Includes accompanying audio.

Tangos for Accordion

A Collection of Traditional Argentine Tangos Arranged for Keyboard Accordion

Born in the impoverished barrios of Buenos Aires during the late 19th Century, the tango has become one of the most important music and dance forms of our time.

Tangos for Accordion presents a distinctive collection of predominantly Argentinian tangos arranged for solo piano accordion. The book's introduction includes a brief history of the tango plus an explanation of tango rhythms (habanera, marcato, etc) and how to perform them on the accordion. Includes many of the best-known tangos, such as La Cumparsita, Caminito, El Choclo, El Marne, Catamarca, La Paloma, and many more. For intermediate to advanced players.

visit David DiGiuseppe's website — www.daviddg.com

100 Irish Tunes for Piano Accordion

From Apples in Winter to The Wise Maid, this collection of Irish jigs, reels, and polkas provides beginning to advanced players with a wealth of traditional Irish music for solo keyboard accordion. With fingerings, ornamentation, left-hand notation, and chord symbols included, this book will allow even the novice accordionist to join in a traditional Irish session. Audio files feature 21 of the book's 100 tunes.

100 Tunes for Piano Accordion

An extensive collection of reels, jigs, hornpipes, and polkas from the French Canadian, Cape Breton, Scottish, Shetland, New England, and southern old time traditions arranged for accordion. Written with the beginner as well as the advanced player in mind, the arrangements are complete with ornamentation, fingerings, left-hand notation, and chord symbols. Appropriate for any G clef instrument.

Favorite Hymns and Gospel Songs for Accordion

A collection of the most-loved, all-time favorite gospel songs and hymns for the keyboard accordion. The songs are presented in easy-to-read arrangements in popular keys, with accompanying fingering suggestions and chord symbols. These short and lyrical arrangements are perfect for use in a worship setting or just for fun.

Wedding Collection for Accordion

This book presents a collection of classic wedding standards for solo keyboard accordion. The songs are presented in easy-to-read arrangements in popular keys. Each piece includes fingering suggestions and a recommendation for placement within the wedding ceremony. Arrangements vary from easy to intermediate.

WWW.MELBAY.COM